MR. FLEMIN

MUSHROOM IDENTIFICATION LOGBOOK

Mushroom Identification Field Guide Record Book

DIY MUSHROOM SERIES

Fleming's

STEPHEN FLEMING

How to use this book

This record book is a part of the DIY Mushroom series from Fleming Publications and is aimed to be your companion while you conduct Mushroom Foraging.

The first few pages give you insight into mushroom anatomy, mushroom tree compatibility, and spore printing technique.

The next part is the logbook which records every minute detail from environment, weather, growth surface, cap, gill, stem, and ring type. Also, one page is provided for spore printing.

The last part of the book contains few blank pages for notes and diagrams. It also includes a glossary for the mushroom hunters for understanding the terminologies involved.

Happy Hunting!

Stephen Fleming

MUSHROOM ANATOMY

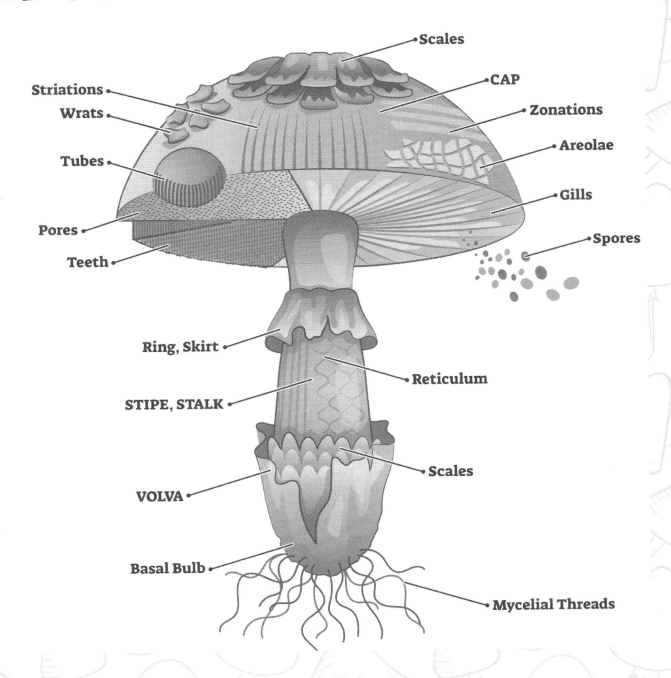

Scales

CAP

Striations

Zonations

Wrats

Areolae

Tubes

Gills

Pores

Spores

Teeth

Ring, Skirt

Reticulum

STIPE, STALK

VOLVA

Scales

Basal Bulb

Mycelial Threads

Mushroom Identification

Identifying mushrooms is challenging, especially for beginners. Difficulties of identification come from the absence of info collected in the field or distinguishing functions on the mushrooms collected.

While collecting and identifying the mushroom, always note :

- Where is the mushroom coming from - This appears simple in the beginning until you are in the complex environment. Typical questions in guides are: What kind of tree was the mushroom discovered growing on? Was the tree living or dead, or is the mushroom growing on the turf, wood chips, dirt, or roots of an old tree.

- In which season was the mushroom collected?

- Are there numerous mushrooms in the area? If multiple mushrooms are available, do they collaborate at the base, or are they separate?

- Is there a distinctive smell around the mushrooms? Some mushrooms have a distinct odor to attract bugs to aid in distributing their spores.

- Be forewarned that some mushrooms will certainly transform colors once they are touched and might melt before you can get them home.

EDIBLE MUSHROOMS SET

CEP

CHAMPIGNONS

AGARIC

OYSTER

SUILLUS

CORAL MILKY CAR

PORCINI

RUSSULA

LACTARIUS

ASPEN

CAESAR'S

MOREL

SAFFRON

SHIITAKE

CHANTERELLE

BLACK TRUFFLE

ENOKI

INDIGO
LACTARIUS

LION'S MANE
MUSHROOM

PUFFBALL

Spore Print

Cut off stem

Put cap on white paper

Remove cap

Wait a few hours...

The Mushroom

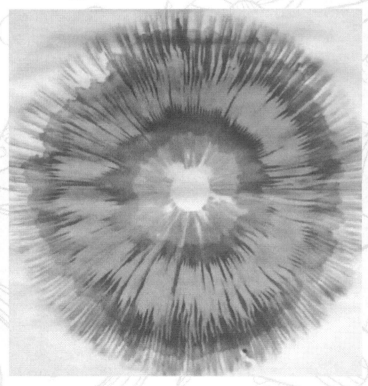

It's Spore Print

Spore Print

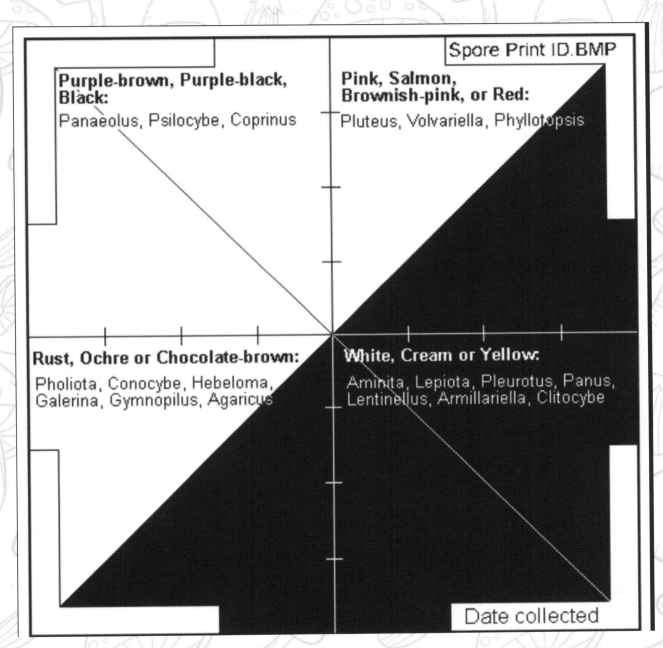

Spore Print ID.BMP

Purple-brown, Purple-black, Black:
Panaeolus, Psilocybe, Coprinus

Pink, Salmon, Brownish-pink, or Red:
Pluteus, Volvariella, Phyllotopsis

Rust, Ochre or Chocolate-brown:
Pholiota, Conocybe, Hebeloma, Galerina, Gymnopilus, Agaricus

White, Cream or Yellow:
Aminita, Lepiota, Pleurotus, Panus, Lentinellus, Armillariella, Clitocybe

Date collected

Mushroom Identification

Mushroom Tree Compatibility

Mushroom Type	Tree Species
Shiitake	Alder,Ash,Beech,Chestnut,Cottonwood,Elm,Eucalyptus,Hickory,Maple,Oaks,Sweetgum
Oyster	Alder,Beech,Birch,Poplar,Elm,Maple,Oaks
Nameko	Alder,Maple,Oaks
Lion's Mane	Chestnut,Poplar/Cottonwood,Elm,Maple,Oaks
Reishi	Poplar/Cottonwood,Elm,Maple,Oaks
Chicken of Woods	Fir,Hemlock,Spruce
Turkey Tail	Alder,Ash,Beech,Chestnut,Cottonwood,Elm,Eucalyptus,Hickory,Maple,Oaks,Sweetgum,Birch,Elm,Fir,Hemlocks,Spruce,Plum,Magnolia,Honey Locust,Willow,Tupelo,Ironwood
Maitake	Poplar,Elm,Honey Locust,Maple,Oaks
King Oyester	Oaks

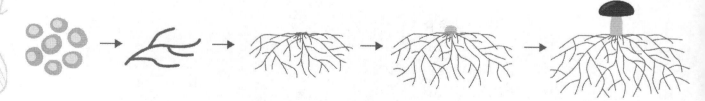

Mushroom life cycle growth mycelium from spore spore germination mycelial expansion and formation

Tips for Beginner's

- If you are 99% sure about any mushroom, don't eat it!

- The one cardinal rule in mushroom hunting is: If in doubt, throw it out.

- Transform into super-familiar with all the different identity features, do not consume something unless you have a 100% identification.

- Begin with straightforward ones before you try to identify much more intricate types.

- Start by just consuming a small amount the first time.

- Identifying mushrooms is all about repeating, practicing, and hands-on instruction.

- You'll require a guide(book/video), training, and some quality time in the woods to get started.

- One of the initial pieces of advice I got was," Learn about poisonous ones first."

- Utilize all your five senses to identify the mushroom.

- Carefully observe all the parts of a mushroom. (Cap, gills, stem, ring, and more).

- Don't be in a hurry; give ample time.

- Always keep in mind the region where you are foraging.

- Take a spore print.

- **Get the correct information based on data:** According to the National Data Poison System, there are around three deaths and about 7500 nausea and organ failure cases due to mushroom consumption.

  So there are basic thumb rules for consuming mushrooms:

- -**Some mushrooms can be deadly (like death cap) and then those which can make you sick. Know about them first.**

- -**The very best way to avoid poisoning is to get accustomed to the characteristics of the certain mushrooms you're searching for, discover when and where they're available.**

- **Never eat a raw mushroom. Always cook before eating.**

HOW TO HARVEST MUSHROOMS CORRECTLY?

Few Poisnous Mushrooms

- **Amanita phalloides or Death Cap**

It is a lethal poisonous fungus widely spread in Europe. They are in charge of 90% of the world's mushroom-related deaths. The caps of these mushrooms are green in the shade, and their stipe and gills are white. The death cap looks like several edible mushrooms, such as the straw mushrooms and the caesar's mushroom, which can cause unintentional poisoning. Remarkable fatalities consist of Pope Clement VII, who died of unintentional death cap poisoning in 1534, and perhaps Roman Emperor Claudius in 54 CE.

Amanita phalloides or Death Cap

- **Destroying Angels**

The ruining angels are a species of toxic white mushrooms in the genus Amanita family. The taxonomic name is Amanita bisporigera. This fungus species lives in eastern as well as western parts of North America and also Europe. The varieties frequently grow near the sides of timberlands and can be found in grassy lawns near trees and bushes. Ingesting also half of a ruining angel mushroom can be deadly otherwise quickly treated. The intake of this fungus brings damages the liver as well as the kidney.

Destroying Angels

- **False Morel**

The false morel is a mushroom species that resembles real morels from the genus Morchella. This species of fungus is medically called Gyromitra esculenta. The mushrooms are recognized to be delicious but dangerous if consumed fresh.

False Morel

- **Autumn Skullcap/ Galerina marginata/Funeral bell**

Spotted around the Northern Hemisphere, the Autumn Skullcap grows on dead timber even in the Arctic and some parts of Australia. They are gilled mushrooms and also look comparable to the edible mushroom species. For this, they have been in charge of numerous human deaths. Individuals commonly confuse Autumn Skullcap with the edible velour foot, covered wood tuft, honey fungus, and also hallucinogenic psilocybe mushrooms.

Autumn Skullcap

- **Death Webcap**

Cortinarius rubellus, commonly called Death Webcap, is one of the most dangerous mushrooms ever found. They have a similar look to many edible mushroom types; however, they possess orellanine toxin. Often, orellanine is misdiagnosed, ultimately resulting in kidney failure and also death.

Death Webcap

- **Fly Agaric**

Fly Agaric, clinically called Amanita Muscaria, is another harmful mushroom variety. With the quickly noticeable bright red cap with white spots, this fungus appears to have straight emerged from a fairytale. It looks eye-catching and spectacular. This is the most iconic toadstool mushroom, and you must have seen it in some form in popular culture or gaming. (Remember Super Mushroom from Super Mario game).

Fly Agaric

General Details

Date/Day Aug. 15, 2022

Weather ☐ ☑ ☐

Location/GPS Cumming F.P.

Temprature 70-80°F.

By/Person Amelie and Mumuchi

Growth Medium & Surrounding

Forest Type ☐ Coniferous ☐ Tropical ☑ Deciduous ☐ Others

Remarks _____

Growth Medium
☑ Soil ☐ Grass ☐ Dead Wood ☐ Tree
☐ Leaf ☐ Rocky Surface ☐ Mushroom ☐ Other

Remarks _____

Soil Type ☐ Clay ☐ Sandy ☑ Loam ☐ Others

Additional Information

Species/Type agaric

Color white

Specimen

Length 1 inch

Cap Shape and Characterstics

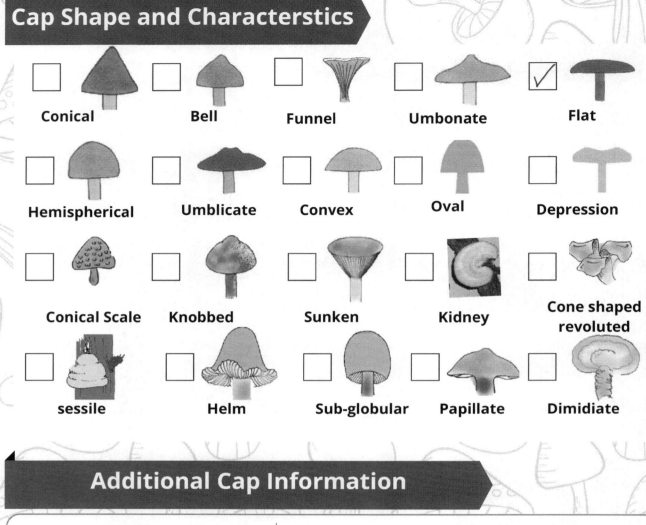

☐ Conical	☐ Bell	☐ Funnel	☐ Umbonate	☑ Flat
☐ Hemispherical	☐ Umblicate	☐ Convex	☐ Oval	☐ Depression
☐ Conical Scale	☐ Knobbed	☐ Sunken	☐ Kidney	Cone shaped revoluted
☐ sessile	☐ Helm	☐ Sub-globular	☐ Papillate	Dimidiate

Additional Cap Information

Cap Diagram

Other details

Cap color   grey

Cap shape   pancake

Cap texture   smooth

Cap diameter   2.5"-3" inch.

Cap length

Hymenium   gills

Cap surface

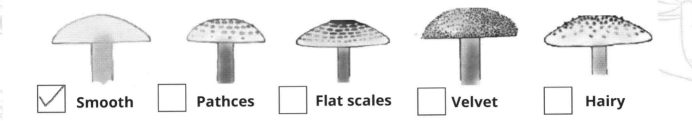

- ☑ Smooth
- ☐ Pathces
- ☐ Flat scales
- ☐ Velvet
- ☐ Hairy

Gills

- ☐ False Gills
- ☐ Teeth
- ☐ Pores
- ☑ Gills

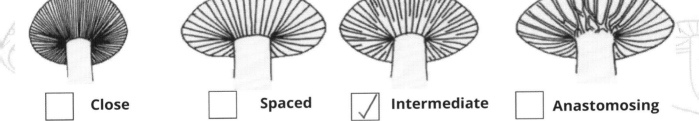

- ☐ Close
- ☐ Spaced
- ☑ Intermediate
- ☐ Anastomosing

Additional Notes

Gill attachment to the stalk

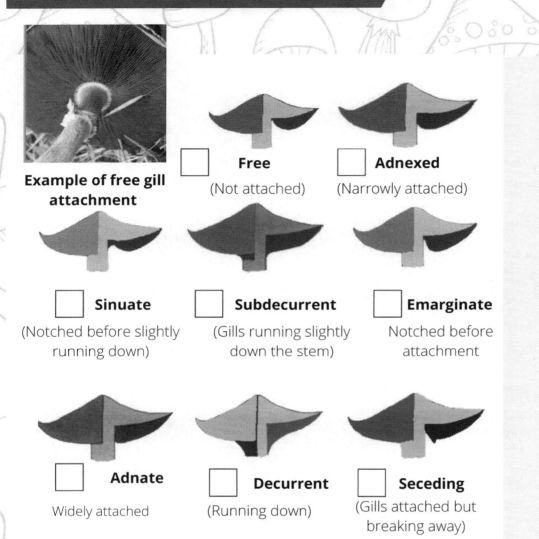

Example of free gill attachment

☐ **Free**
(Not attached)

☐ **Adnexed**
(Narrowly attached)

☐ **Sinuate**
(Notched before slightly running down)

☐ **Subdecurrent**
(Gills running slightly down the stem)

☐ **Emarginate**
Notched before attachment

☐ **Adnate**
Widely attached

☐ **Decurrent**
(Running down)

☐ **Seceding**
(Gills attached but breaking away)

Sketch

Additional Notes

Stem Shape

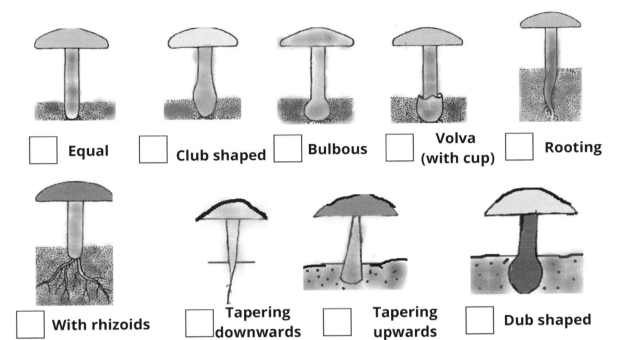

- [ ] Equal
- [ ] Club shaped
- [ ] Bulbous
- [ ] Volva (with cup)
- [ ] Rooting
- [ ] With rhizoids
- [ ] Tapering downwards
- [ ] Tapering upwards
- [ ] Dub shaped

Mushroom Ring Type

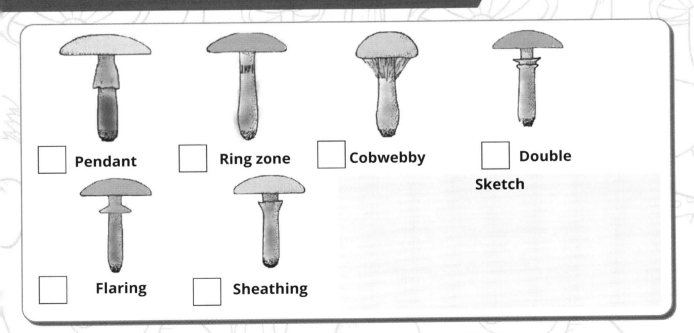

- [ ] Pendant
- [ ] Ring zone
- [ ] Cobwebby
- [ ] Double
- [ ] Flaring
- [ ] Sheathing

Sketch

Spore Print

Mushroom Species:_____

DATE: / /	**WEATHER:**	**LOCATION:**
SUBSTRATE:	Detail:	
SOIL:	**VEGETATION:**	
Recent weather:		

General Details

Date/Day _____

Weather ☐ ☐ ☐

Location/GPS _____

Temprature _____

By/Person _____

Growth Medium & Surrounding

Forest Type

☐ Coniferous ☐ Tropical ☐ Deciduous ☐ Others

Remarks _____

Growth Medium

☐ Soil ☐ Grass ☐ Dead Wood ☐ Tree

☐ Leaf ☐ Rocky Surface ☐ Mushroom ☐ Other

Remarks _____

Soil Type

☐ Clay ☐ Sandy ☐ Loam ☐ Others

Additional Information

Species/Type _____

Color _____

Specimen _____

Length _____

Cap Shape and Characterstics

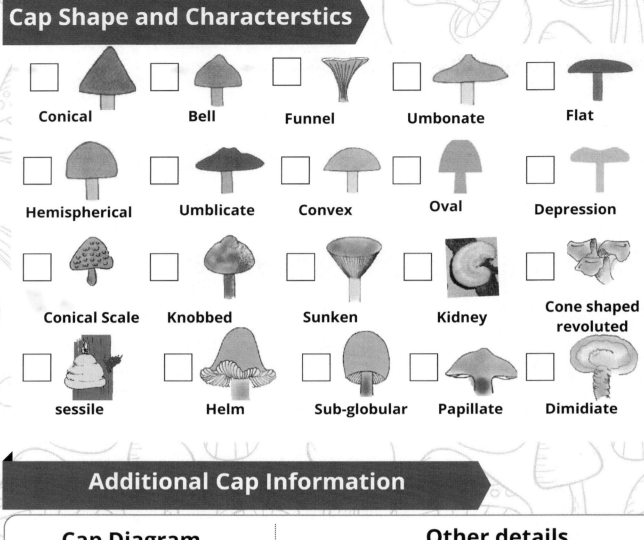

☐ Conical

☐ Bell

☐ Funnel

☐ Umbonate

☐ Flat

☐ Hemispherical

☐ Umblicate

☐ Convex

☐ Oval

☐ Depression

☐ Conical Scale

☐ Knobbed

☐ Sunken

☐ Kidney

☐ Cone shaped revoluted

☐ sessile

☐ Helm

☐ Sub-globular

☐ Papillate

☐ Dimidiate

Additional Cap Information

Cap Diagram

Other details

Cap color ....

Cap shape ....

Cap texture ....

Cap diameter ....

Cap length ....

Hymenium ....

Cap surface

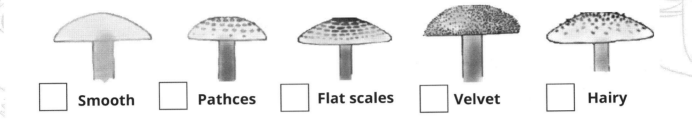

☐ Smooth ☐ Pathces ☐ Flat scales ☐ Velvet ☐ Hairy

Gills

☐ False Gills ☐ Teeth ☐ Pores ☐ Gills

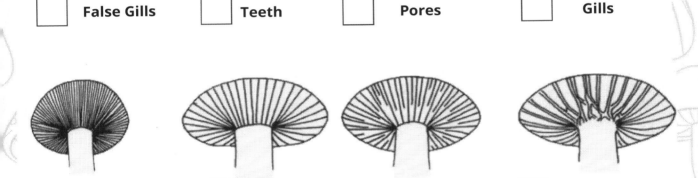

☐ Close ☐ Spaced ☐ Intermediate ☐ Anastomosing

Additional Notes

Gill attachment to the stalk

Sketch

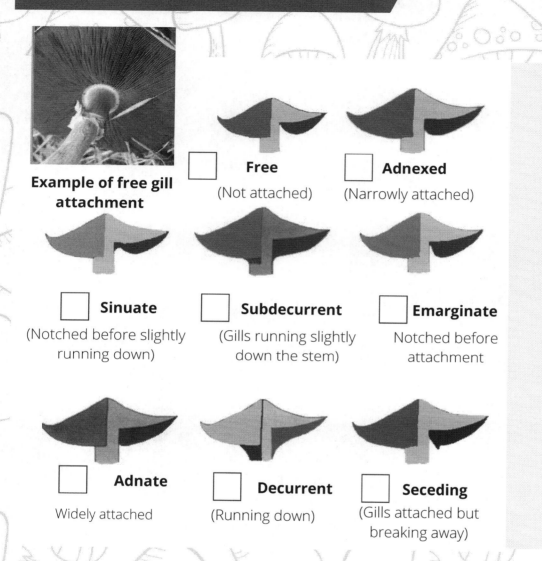

Example of free gill attachment

☐ **Free** (Not attached)

☐ **Adnexed** (Narrowly attached)

☐ **Sinuate** (Notched before slightly running down)

☐ **Subdecurrent** (Gills running slightly down the stem)

☐ **Emarginate** Notched before attachment

☐ **Adnate** Widely attached

☐ **Decurrent** (Running down)

☐ **Seceding** (Gills attached but breaking away)

Additional Notes

Stem Shape

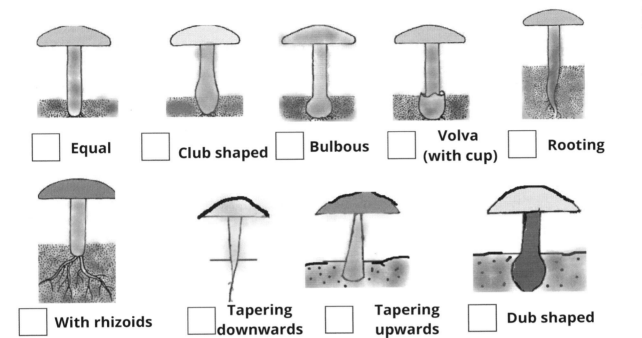

☐ Equal ☐ Club shaped ☐ Bulbous ☐ Volva (with cup) ☐ Rooting

☐ With rhizoids ☐ Tapering downwards ☐ Tapering upwards ☐ Dub shaped

Mushroom Ring Type

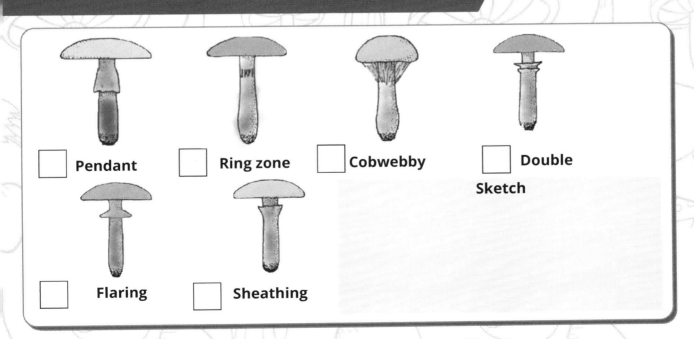

☐ Pendant ☐ Ring zone ☐ Cobwebby ☐ Double

Sketch

☐ Flaring ☐ Sheathing

Spore Print

Mushroom Species:_____

DATE: / /	WEATHER:	LOCATION:

SUBSTRATE: Detail:

SOIL: **VEGETATION:**

Recent weather:

General Details

📅 Date/Day _____

☀️ Weather ☐ ⛅ ☐ 🌧️ ☐

📍 Location/GPS _____

🌡️ Temprature _____

👤 By/Person _____

Growth Medium & Surrounding

Forest Type
☐ Coniferous ☐ Tropical ☐ Deciduous ☐ Others

Remarks _____

Growth Medium
☐ Soil ☐ Grass ☐ Dead Wood ☐ Tree
☐ Leaf ☐ Rocky Surface ☐ Mushroom ☐ Other

Remarks _____

Soil Type
☐ Clay ☐ Sandy ☐ Loam ☐ Others

Additional Information

Species/Type _____   Color _____

Specimen _____   Length _____

Cap Shape and Characterstics

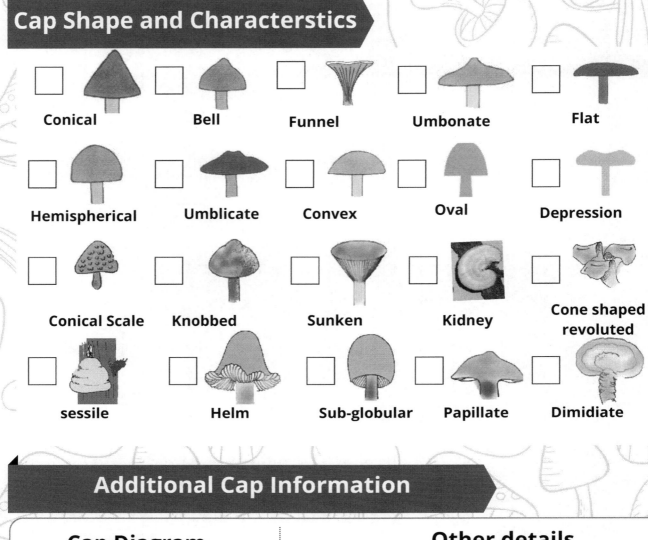

☐ Conical
☐ Bell
☐ Funnel
☐ Umbonate
☐ Flat

☐ Hemispherical
☐ Umblicate
☐ Convex
☐ Oval
☐ Depression

☐ Conical Scale
☐ Knobbed
☐ Sunken
☐ Kidney
☐ Cone shaped revoluted

☐ sessile
☐ Helm
☐ Sub-globular
☐ Papillate
☐ Dimidiate

Additional Cap Information

Cap Diagram

Other details

Cap color ....

Cap shape ....

Cap texture ....

Cap diameter ....

Cap length ....

Hymenium ....

Cap surface

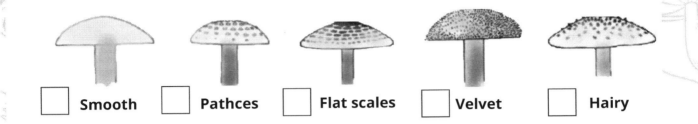

- ☐ Smooth
- ☐ Pathces
- ☐ Flat scales
- ☐ Velvet
- ☐ Hairy

Gills

- ☐ False Gills
- ☐ Teeth
- ☐ Pores
- ☐ Gills

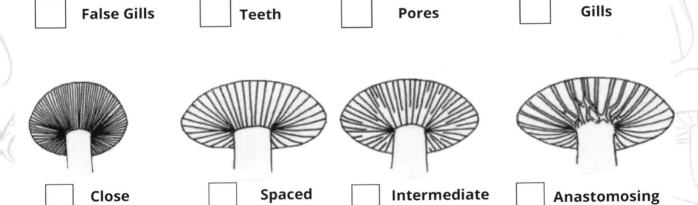

- ☐ Close
- ☐ Spaced
- ☐ Intermediate
- ☐ Anastomosing

Additional Notes

Gill attachment to the stalk

Sketch

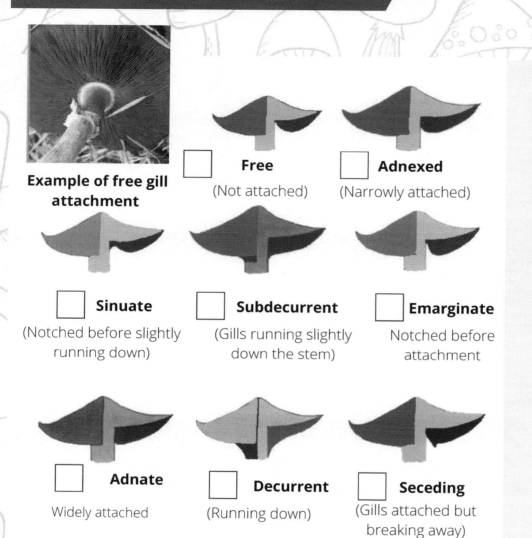

Example of free gill attachment

☐ **Free**
(Not attached)

☐ **Adnexed**
(Narrowly attached)

☐ **Sinuate**
(Notched before slightly running down)

☐ **Subdecurrent**
(Gills running slightly down the stem)

☐ **Emarginate**
Notched before attachment

☐ **Adnate**
Widely attached

☐ **Decurrent**
(Running down)

☐ **Seceding**
(Gills attached but breaking away)

Additional Notes

Stem Shape

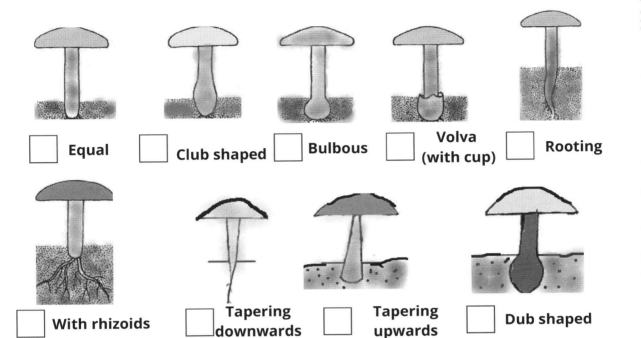

- [ ] Equal
- [ ] Club shaped
- [ ] Bulbous
- [ ] Volva (with cup)
- [ ] Rooting
- [ ] With rhizoids
- [ ] Tapering downwards
- [ ] Tapering upwards
- [ ] Dub shaped

Mushroom Ring Type

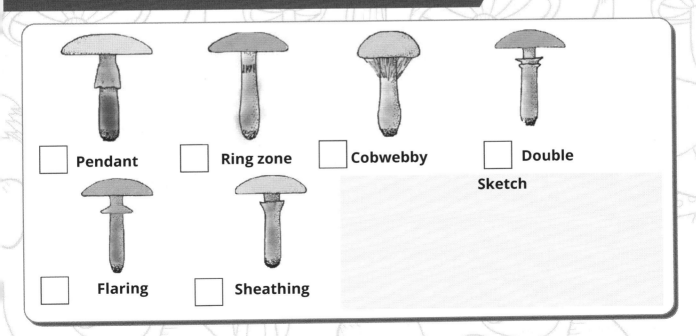

- [ ] Pendant
- [ ] Ring zone
- [ ] Cobwebby
- [ ] Double
- [ ] Flaring
- [ ] Sheathing

Sketch

Spore Print

Mushroom Species:_____

| DATE: /   / | WEATHER: | LOCATION: |

SUBSTRATE: Detail:

SOIL: **VEGETATION:**

Recent weather:

General Details

📅 _____
Date/Day

Weather ☐ ☐ ☐

📍 _____
Location/GPS

🌡 _____
Temprature

👤 _____
By/Person

Growth Medium & Surrounding

☐ **Coniferous** ☐ **Tropical** ☐ **Deciduous** ☐ **Others**

Forest Type **Remarks** _____

☐ **Soil** ☐ **Grass** ☐ **Dead Wood** ☐ **Tree**

☐ **Leaf** ☐ **Rocky Surface** ☐ **Mushroom** ☐ **Other**

Growth Medium

Remarks _____

☐ **Clay** ☐ **Sandy** ☐ **Loam** ☐ **Others**

Soil Type

Additional Information

Species/Type _____ **Color** _____

Specimen _____ **Length** _____

Cap Shape and Characterstics

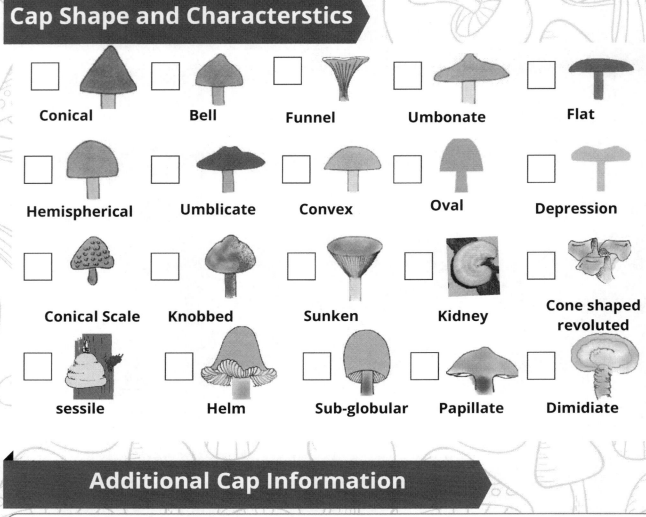

- ☐ Conical
- ☐ Bell
- ☐ Funnel
- ☐ Umbonate
- ☐ Flat
- ☐ Hemispherical
- ☐ Umblicate
- ☐ Convex
- ☐ Oval
- ☐ Depression
- ☐ Conical Scale
- ☐ Knobbed
- ☐ Sunken
- ☐ Kidney
- ☐ Cone shaped revoluted
- ☐ sessile
- ☐ Helm
- ☐ Sub-globular
- ☐ Papillate
- ☐ Dimidiate

Additional Cap Information

Cap Diagram

Other details

Cap color ....

Cap shape ....

Cap texture ....

Cap diameter ....

Cap length ....

Hymenium ....

Cap surface

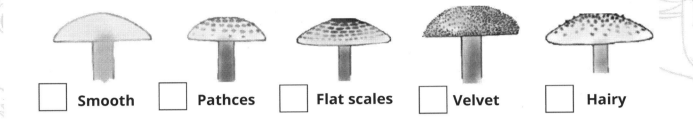

☐ Smooth ☐ Pathces ☐ Flat scales ☐ Velvet ☐ Hairy

Gills

☐ False Gills ☐ Teeth ☐ Pores ☐ Gills

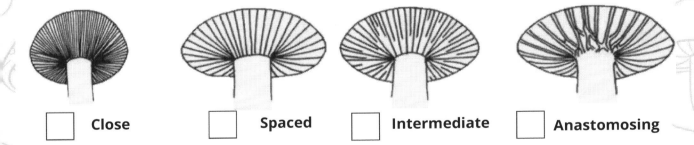

☐ Close ☐ Spaced ☐ Intermediate ☐ Anastomosing

Additional Notes

Gill attachment to the stalk

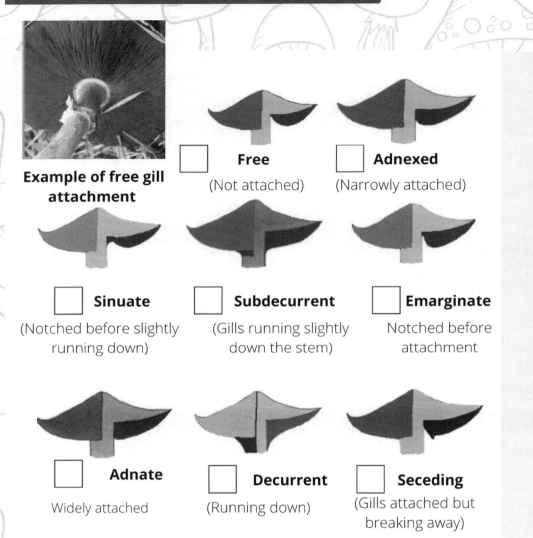

Example of free gill attachment

☐ **Free**
(Not attached)

☐ **Adnexed**
(Narrowly attached)

☐ **Sinuate**
(Notched before slightly running down)

☐ **Subdecurrent**
(Gills running slightly down the stem)

☐ **Emarginate**
Notched before attachment

☐ **Adnate**
Widely attached

☐ **Decurrent**
(Running down)

☐ **Seceding**
(Gills attached but breaking away)

Sketch

Additional Notes

Stem Shape

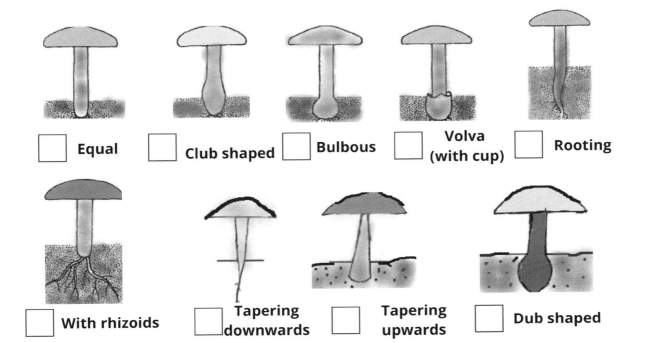

☐ Equal ☐ Club shaped ☐ Bulbous ☐ Volva (with cup) ☐ Rooting

☐ With rhizoids ☐ Tapering downwards ☐ Tapering upwards ☐ Dub shaped

Mushroom Ring Type

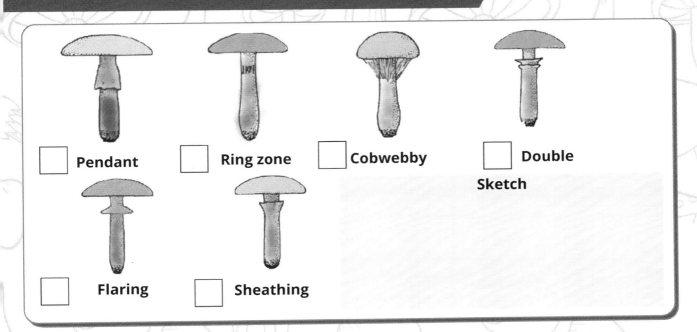

☐ Pendant ☐ Ring zone ☐ Cobwebby ☐ Double

Sketch

☐ Flaring ☐ Sheathing

Spore Print

Mushroom Species:_____

DATE: / /	**WEATHER:**	**LOCATION:**
SUBSTRATE:	Detail:	
SOIL:	**VEGETATION:**	
Recent weather:		

General Details

Date/Day _ _ _ _ _ _ _ _ _ _ _

Weather ☐ ☐ ☐

Location/GPS _ _ _ _ _ _ _ _ _ _

Temprature _ _ _ _ _ _ _ _

By/Person _ _ _ _ _ _ _ _

Growth Medium & Surrounding

Forest Type
☐ Coniferous ☐ Tropical ☐ Deciduous ☐ Others

Remarks _

Growth Medium
☐ Soil ☐ Grass ☐ Dead Wood ☐ Tree
☐ Leaf ☐ Rocky Surface ☐ Mushroom ☐ Other

Remarks _

Soil Type
☐ Clay ☐ Sandy ☐ Loam ☐ Others

Additional Information

Species/Type _ _ _ _ _ _ _ _ _ _ _ _ _

Color _ _ _ _ _ _ _ _ _ _ _ _

Specimen _ _ _ _ _ _ _ _ _ _ _ _

Length _ _ _ _ _ _ _ _ _ _ _ _

Cap Shape and Characterstics

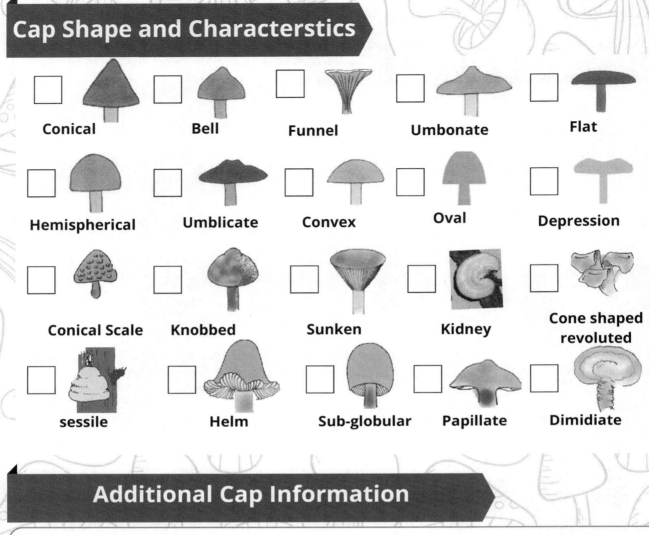

☐ Conical
☐ Bell
☐ Funnel
☐ Umbonate
☐ Flat

☐ Hemispherical
☐ Umblicate
☐ Convex
☐ Oval
☐ Depression

☐ Conical Scale
☐ Knobbed
☐ Sunken
☐ Kidney
☐ Cone shaped revoluted

☐ sessile
☐ Helm
☐ Sub-globular
☐ Papillate
☐ Dimidiate

Additional Cap Information

Cap Diagram

Other details

Cap color ....

Cap shape ....

Cap texture ....

Cap diameter ....

Cap length ....

Hymenium ....

Cap surface

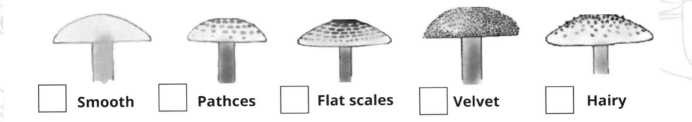

☐ Smooth ☐ Pathces ☐ Flat scales ☐ Velvet ☐ Hairy

Gills

☐ False Gills ☐ Teeth ☐ Pores ☐ Gills

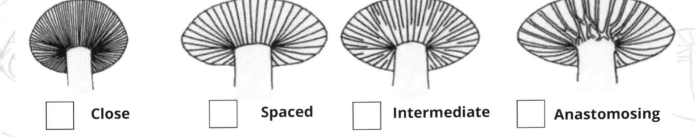

☐ Close ☐ Spaced ☐ Intermediate ☐ Anastomosing

Additional Notes

Gill attachment to the stalk

Example of free gill attachment

☐ **Free**
(Not attached)

☐ **Adnexed**
(Narrowly attached)

☐ **Sinuate**
(Notched before slightly running down)

☐ **Subdecurrent**
(Gills running slightly down the stem)

☐ **Emarginate**
Notched before attachment

☐ **Adnate**
Widely attached

☐ **Decurrent**
(Running down)

☐ **Seceding**
(Gills attached but breaking away)

Additional Notes

Stem Shape

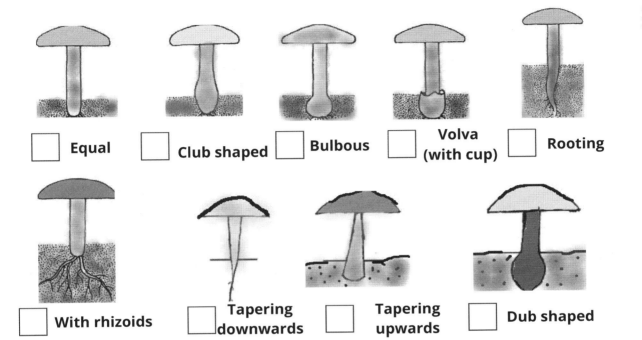

- [ ] Equal
- [ ] Club shaped
- [ ] Bulbous
- [ ] Volva (with cup)
- [ ] Rooting
- [ ] With rhizoids
- [ ] Tapering downwards
- [ ] Tapering upwards
- [ ] Dub shaped

Mushroom Ring Type

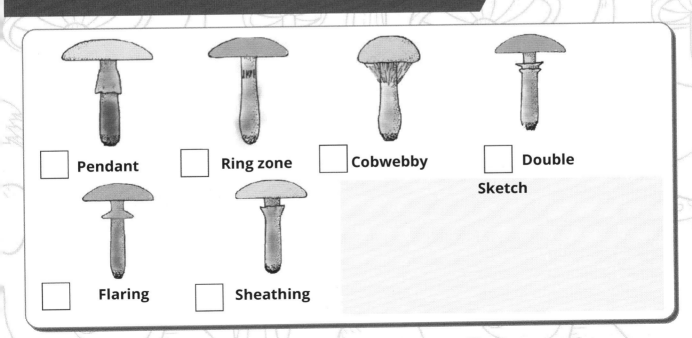

- [ ] Pendant
- [ ] Ring zone
- [ ] Cobwebby
- [ ] Double
- [ ] Flaring
- [ ] Sheathing

Sketch

Spore Print

Mushroom Species:_____

DATE: / /	**WEATHER:**	**LOCATION:**

SUBSTRATE: Detail:

SOIL: **VEGETATION:**

Recent weather:

General Details

Date/Day _____

Weather ☐ ☐ ☐

Location/GPS _____

Temprature _____

By/Person _____

Growth Medium & Surrounding

Forest Type
☐ Coniferous   ☐ Tropical   ☐ Deciduous   ☐ Others

Remarks _____

Growth Medium
☐ Soil   ☐ Grass   ☐ Dead Wood   ☐ Tree
☐ Leaf   ☐ Rocky Surface   ☐ Mushroom   ☐ Other

Remarks _____

Soil Type
☐ Clay   ☐ Sandy   ☐ Loam   ☐ Others

Additional Information

Species/Type _____

Color _____

Specimen _____

Length _____

Cap Shape and Characterstics

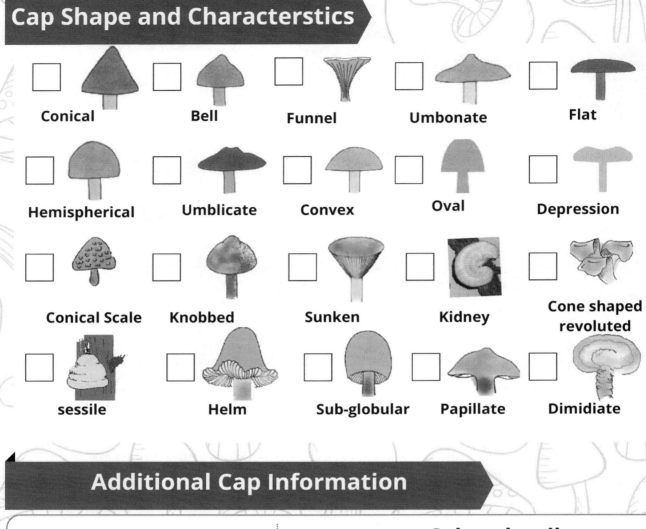

☐ Conical
☐ Bell
☐ Funnel
☐ Umbonate
☐ Flat

☐ Hemispherical
☐ Umblicate
☐ Convex
☐ Oval
☐ Depression

☐ Conical Scale
☐ Knobbed
☐ Sunken
☐ Kidney
☐ Cone shaped revoluted

☐ sessile
☐ Helm
☐ Sub-globular
☐ Papillate
☐ Dimidiate

Additional Cap Information

Cap Diagram

Other details

Cap color ....

Cap shape ....

Cap texture ....

Cap diameter ....

Cap length ....

Hymenium ....

Cap surface

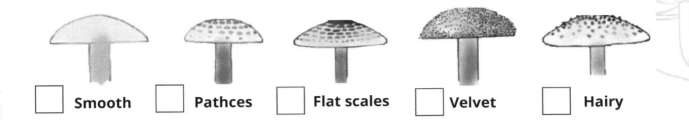

☐ Smooth   ☐ Pathces   ☐ Flat scales   ☐ Velvet   ☐ Hairy

Gills

☐ False Gills   ☐ Teeth   ☐ Pores   ☐ Gills

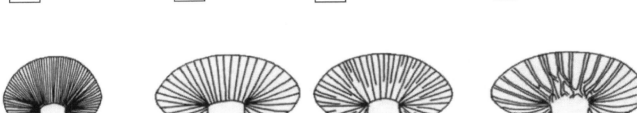

☐ Close   ☐ Spaced   ☐ Intermediate   ☐ Anastomosing

Additional Notes

Gill attachment to the stalk

Example of free gill attachment

☐ **Free**
(Not attached)

☐ **Adnexed**
(Narrowly attached)

☐ **Sinuate**
(Notched before slightly running down)

☐ **Subdecurrent**
(Gills running slightly down the stem)

☐ **Emarginate**
Notched before attachment

☐ **Adnate**
Widely attached

☐ **Decurrent**
(Running down)

☐ **Seceding**
(Gills attached but breaking away)

Additional Notes

Stem Shape

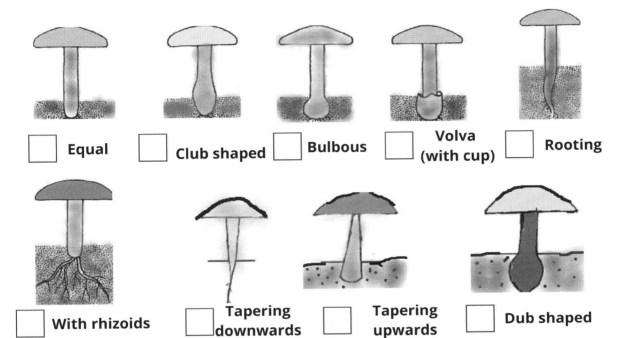

☐ Equal ☐ Club shaped ☐ Bulbous ☐ Volva (with cup) ☐ Rooting

☐ With rhizoids ☐ Tapering downwards ☐ Tapering upwards ☐ Dub shaped

Mushroom Ring Type

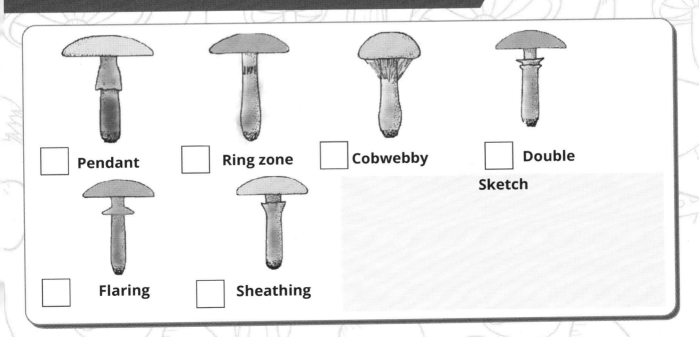

☐ Pendant ☐ Ring zone ☐ Cobwebby ☐ Double

Sketch

☐ Flaring ☐ Sheathing

Spore Print

Mushroom Species:_____

DATE: / /	**WEATHER:**	**LOCATION:**

SUBSTRATE: Detail:

SOIL: **VEGETATION:**

Recent weather:

General Details

Date/Day _____

Weather

☐ ☐ ☐

Location/GPS _____

Temprature _____

By/Person _____

Growth Medium & Surrounding

Forest Type

☐ Coniferous ☐ Tropical ☐ Deciduous ☐ Others

Remarks _____

Growth Medium

☐ Soil ☐ Grass ☐ Dead Wood ☐ Tree

☐ Leaf ☐ Rocky Surface ☐ Mushroom ☐ Other

Remarks _____

Soil Type

☐ Clay ☐ Sandy ☐ Loam ☐ Others

Additional Information

Species/Type _____   **Color** _____

Specimen _____   **Length** _____

Cap Shape and Characterstics

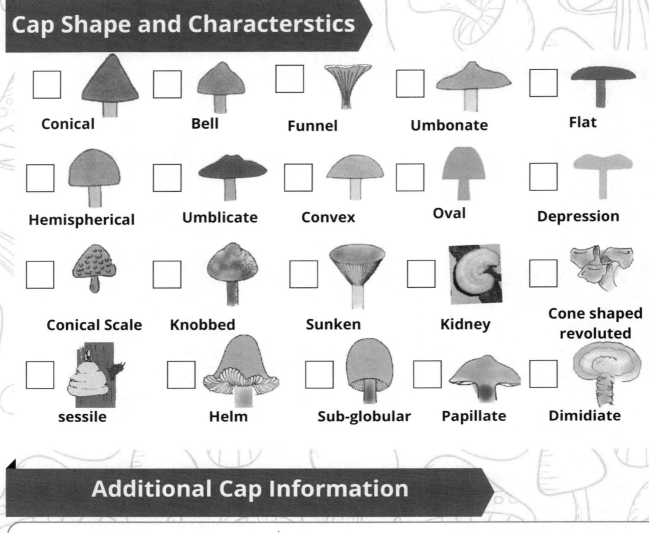

☐ Conical

☐ Bell

☐ Funnel

☐ Umbonate

☐ Flat

☐ Hemispherical

☐ Umblicate

☐ Convex

☐ Oval

☐ Depression

☐ Conical Scale

☐ Knobbed

☐ Sunken

☐ Kidney

☐ Cone shaped revoluted

☐ sessile

☐ Helm

☐ Sub-globular

☐ Papillate

☐ Dimidiate

Additional Cap Information

Cap Diagram

Other details

Cap color ....

Cap shape ....

Cap texture ....

Cap diameter ....

Cap length ....

Hymenium ....

Cap surface

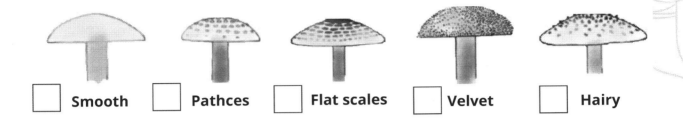

- [ ] Smooth
- [ ] Pathces
- [ ] Flat scales
- [ ] Velvet
- [ ] Hairy

Gills

- [ ] False Gills
- [ ] Teeth
- [ ] Pores
- [ ] Gills

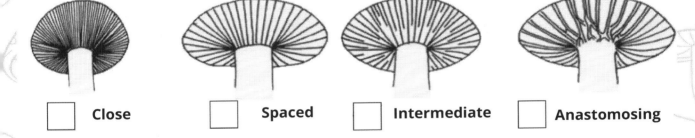

- [ ] Close
- [ ] Spaced
- [ ] Intermediate
- [ ] Anastomosing

Additional Notes

Gill attachment to the stalk

Sketch

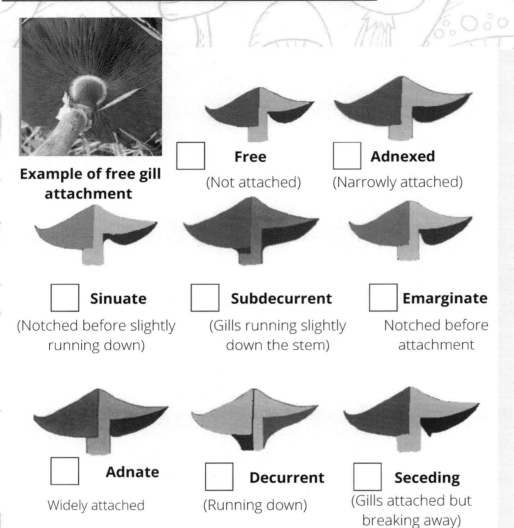

Example of free gill attachment

☐ **Free**
(Not attached)

☐ **Adnexed**
(Narrowly attached)

☐ **Sinuate**
(Notched before slightly running down)

☐ **Subdecurrent**
(Gills running slightly down the stem)

☐ **Emarginate**
Notched before attachment

☐ **Adnate**
Widely attached

☐ **Decurrent**
(Running down)

☐ **Seceding**
(Gills attached but breaking away)

Additional Notes

Stem Shape

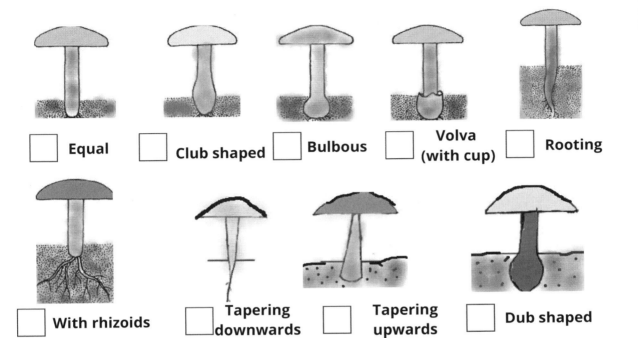

- ☐ Equal
- ☐ Club shaped
- ☐ Bulbous
- ☐ Volva (with cup)
- ☐ Rooting
- ☐ With rhizoids
- ☐ Tapering downwards
- ☐ Tapering upwards
- ☐ Dub shaped

Mushroom Ring Type

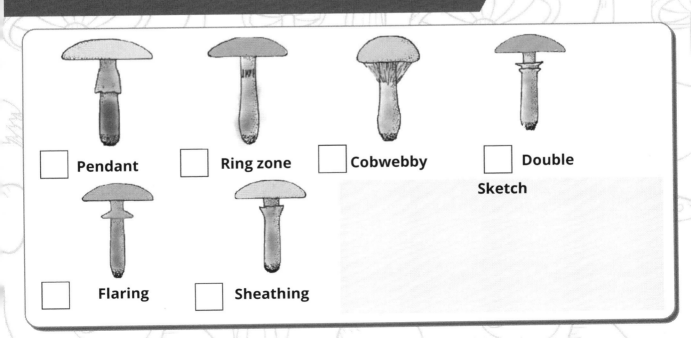

- ☐ Pendant
- ☐ Ring zone
- ☐ Cobwebby
- ☐ Double

Sketch

- ☐ Flaring
- ☐ Sheathing

Spore Print

Mushroom Species:_____

DATE: / /	WEATHER:	LOCATION:

SUBSTRATE:	Detail:

SOIL:	VEGETATION:

Recent weather:

General Details

📅 Date/Day _____

☀️ ☐ ⛅ ☐ 🌧️ ☐ Weather

📍 Location/GPS _____

🌡️ _____ Temprature

👤 _____ By/Person

Growth Medium & Surrounding

Forest Type

☐ Coniferous ☐ Tropical ☐ Deciduous ☐ Others

Remarks _____

Growth Medium

☐ Soil ☐ Grass ☐ Dead Wood ☐ Tree

☐ Leaf ☐ Rocky Surface ☐ Mushroom ☐ Other

Remarks _____

Soil Type

☐ Clay ☐ Sandy ☐ Loam ☐ Others

Additional Information

Species/Type _____

Color _____

Specimen _____

Length _____

Cap Shape and Characterstics

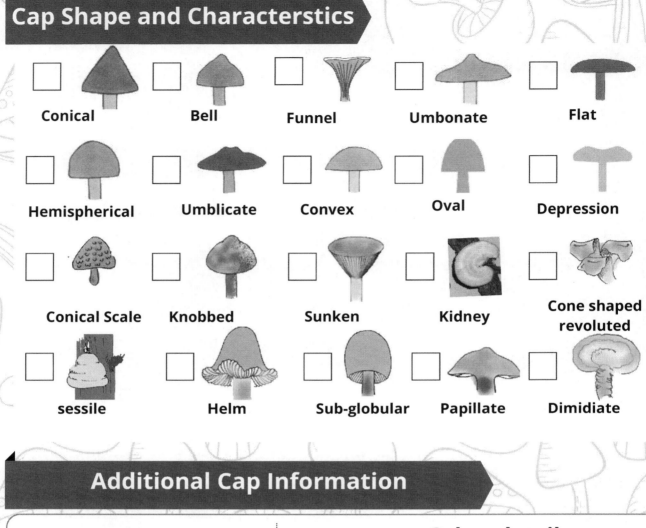

- ☐ Conical
- ☐ Bell
- ☐ Funnel
- ☐ Umbonate
- ☐ Flat
- ☐ Hemispherical
- ☐ Umblicate
- ☐ Convex
- ☐ Oval
- ☐ Depression
- ☐ Conical Scale
- ☐ Knobbed
- ☐ Sunken
- ☐ Kidney
- ☐ Cone shaped revoluted
- ☐ sessile
- ☐ Helm
- ☐ Sub-globular
- ☐ Papillate
- ☐ Dimidiate

Additional Cap Information

Cap Diagram

Other details

Cap color ....

Cap shape ....

Cap texture ....

Cap diameter ....

Cap length ....

Hymenium ....

Cap surface

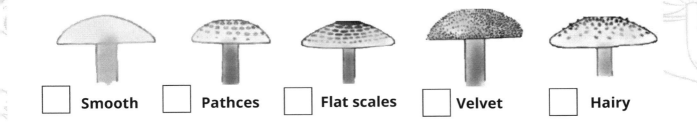

☐ Smooth ☐ Pathces ☐ Flat scales ☐ Velvet ☐ Hairy

Gills

☐ False Gills ☐ Teeth ☐ Pores ☐ Gills

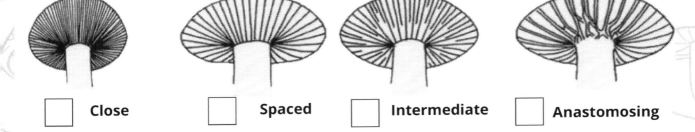

☐ Close ☐ Spaced ☐ Intermediate ☐ Anastomosing

Additional Notes

Gill attachment to the stalk

Sketch

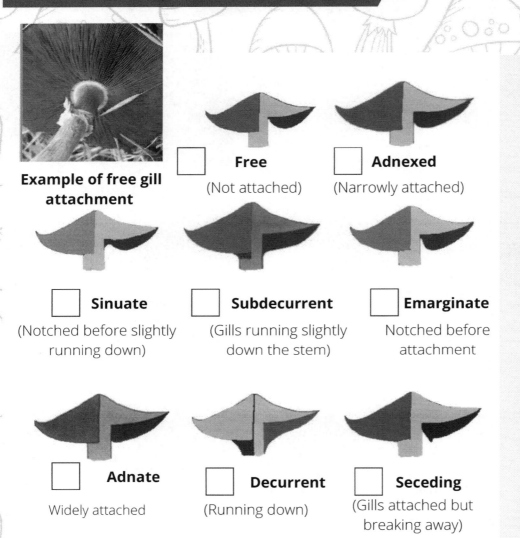

Example of free gill attachment

- [ ] **Free** (Not attached)
- [ ] **Adnexed** (Narrowly attached)
- [ ] **Sinuate** (Notched before slightly running down)
- [ ] **Subdecurrent** (Gills running slightly down the stem)
- [ ] **Emarginate** Notched before attachment
- [ ] **Adnate** Widely attached
- [ ] **Decurrent** (Running down)
- [ ] **Seceding** (Gills attached but breaking away)

Additional Notes

Stem Shape

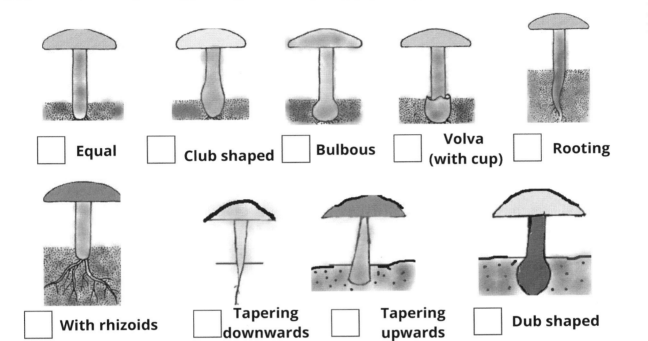

☐ Equal

☐ Club shaped

☐ Bulbous

☐ Volva (with cup)

☐ Rooting

☐ With rhizoids

☐ Tapering downwards

☐ Tapering upwards

☐ Dub shaped

Mushroom Ring Type

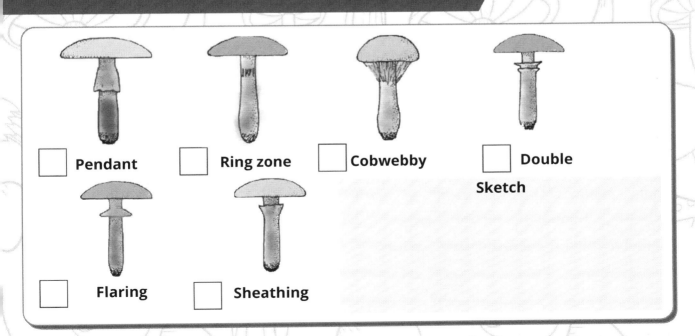

☐ Pendant

☐ Ring zone

☐ Cobwebby

☐ Double

Sketch

☐ Flaring

☐ Sheathing

Spore Print

Mushroom Species:_____

DATE: / /	WEATHER:	LOCATION:

SUBSTRATE: Detail:

SOIL: **VEGETATION:**

Recent weather:

General Details

Date/Day _____

Weather ☐ ☐ ☐

Location/GPS _____

Temprature _____

By/Person _____

Growth Medium & Surrounding

Forest Type
☐ Coniferous ☐ Tropical ☐ Deciduous ☐ Others

Remarks _____

Growth Medium
☐ Soil ☐ Grass ☐ Dead Wood ☐ Tree
☐ Leaf ☐ Rocky Surface ☐ Mushroom ☐ Other

Remarks _____

Soil Type
☐ Clay ☐ Sandy ☐ Loam ☐ Others

Additional Information

Species/Type _____   **Color** _____

Specimen _____   **Length** _____

Cap Shape and Characterstics

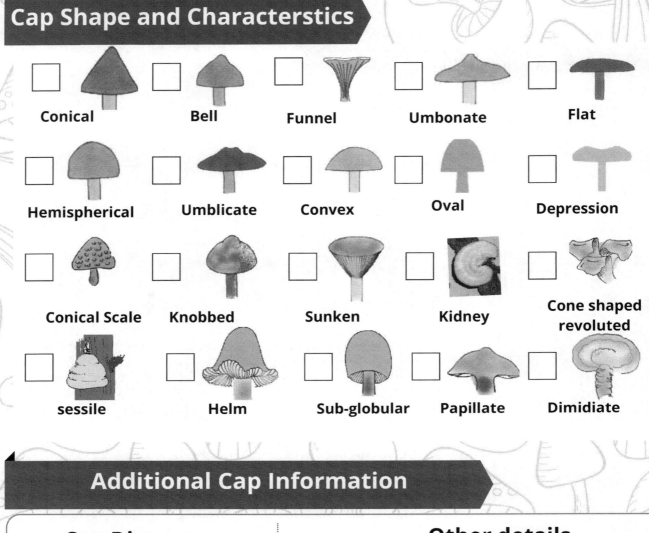

☐ Conical ☐ Bell ☐ Funnel ☐ Umbonate ☐ Flat

☐ Hemispherical ☐ Umblicate ☐ Convex ☐ Oval ☐ Depression

☐ Conical Scale ☐ Knobbed ☐ Sunken ☐ Kidney ☐ Cone shaped revoluted

☐ sessile ☐ Helm ☐ Sub-globular ☐ Papillate ☐ Dimidiate

Additional Cap Information

Cap Diagram

Other details

Cap color ....

Cap shape ....

Cap texture ....

Cap diameter ....

Cap length ....

Hymenium ....

Cap surface

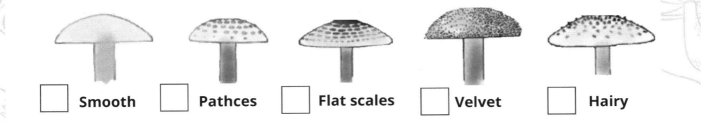

☐ Smooth   ☐ Pathces   ☐ Flat scales   ☐ Velvet   ☐ Hairy

Gills

☐ False Gills   ☐ Teeth   ☐ Pores   ☐ Gills

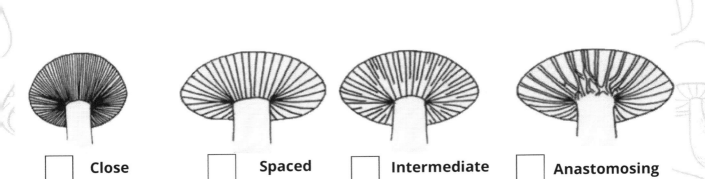

☐ Close   ☐ Spaced   ☐ Intermediate   ☐ Anastomosing

Additional Notes

Gill attachment to the stalk

Sketch

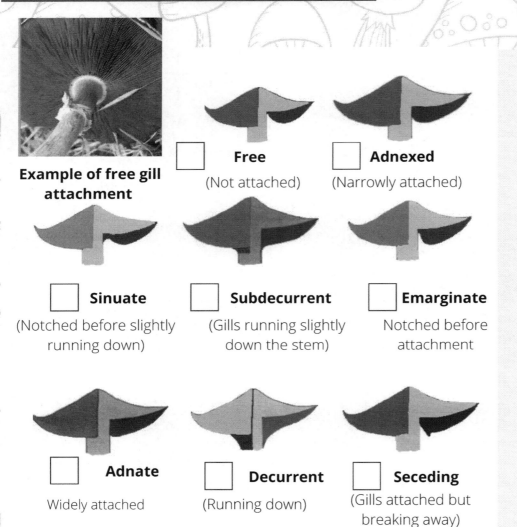

Example of free gill attachment

☐ **Free**
(Not attached)

☐ **Adnexed**
(Narrowly attached)

☐ **Sinuate**
(Notched before slightly running down)

☐ **Subdecurrent**
(Gills running slightly down the stem)

☐ **Emarginate**
Notched before attachment

☐ **Adnate**
Widely attached

☐ **Decurrent**
(Running down)

☐ **Seceding**
(Gills attached but breaking away)

Additional Notes

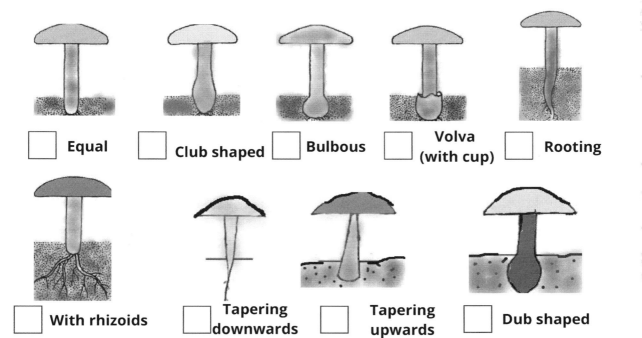

☐ **Equal**　☐ **Club shaped**　☐ **Bulbous**　☐ **Volva (with cup)**　☐ **Rooting**

☐ **With rhizoids**　☐ **Tapering downwards**　☐ **Tapering upwards**　☐ **Dub shaped**

Mushroom Ring Type

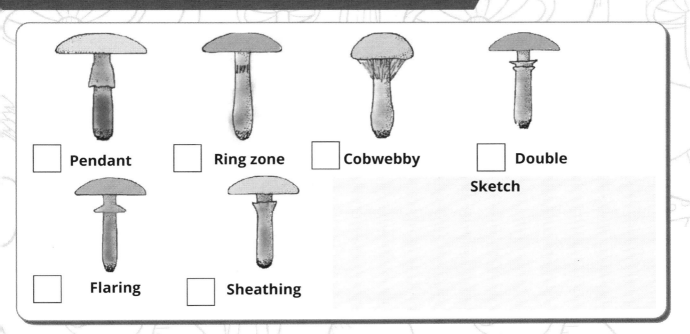

☐ **Pendant**　☐ **Ring zone**　☐ **Cobwebby**　☐ **Double**

Sketch

☐ **Flaring**　☐ **Sheathing**

Spore Print

Mushroom Species:_____

DATE: / /	WEATHER:	LOCATION:

SUBSTRATE: Detail:

SOIL: **VEGETATION:**

Recent weather:

General Details

Date/Day _____

Weather ☐ ☐ ☐

Location/GPS _____

Temprature _____

By/Person _____

Growth Medium & Surrounding

Forest Type
☐ Coniferous   ☐ Tropical   ☐ Deciduous   ☐ Others

Remarks _____

Growth Medium
☐ Soil   ☐ Grass   ☐ Dead Wood   ☐ Tree
☐ Leaf   ☐ Rocky Surface   ☐ Mushroom   ☐ Other

Remarks _____

Soil Type
☐ Clay   ☐ Sandy   ☐ Loam   ☐ Others

Additional Information

Species/Type _____

Color _____

Specimen _____

Length _____

Cap Shape and Characterstics

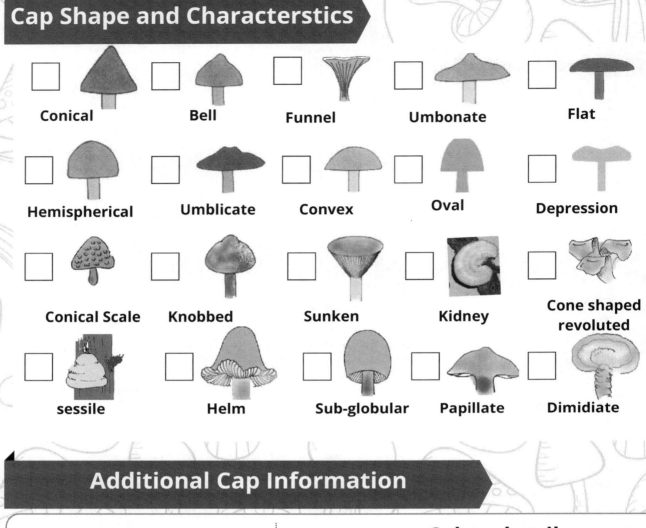

☐ Conical ☐ Bell ☐ Funnel ☐ Umbonate ☐ Flat

☐ Hemispherical ☐ Umblicate ☐ Convex ☐ Oval ☐ Depression

☐ Conical Scale ☐ Knobbed ☐ Sunken ☐ Kidney ☐ Cone shaped revoluted

☐ sessile ☐ Helm ☐ Sub-globular ☐ Papillate ☐ Dimidiate

Additional Cap Information

Cap Diagram

Other details

Cap color ....

Cap shape ....

Cap texture ....

Cap diameter ....

Cap length ....

Hymenium ....

Cap surface

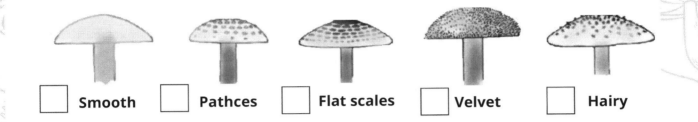

☐ Smooth ☐ Pathces ☐ Flat scales ☐ Velvet ☐ Hairy

Gills

☐ False Gills ☐ Teeth ☐ Pores ☐ Gills

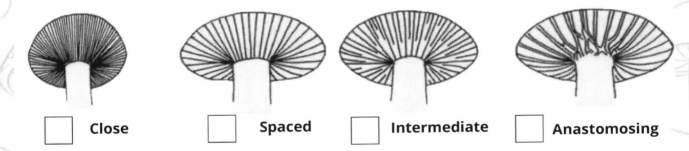

☐ Close ☐ Spaced ☐ Intermediate ☐ Anastomosing

Additional Notes

Gill attachment to the stalk

Sketch

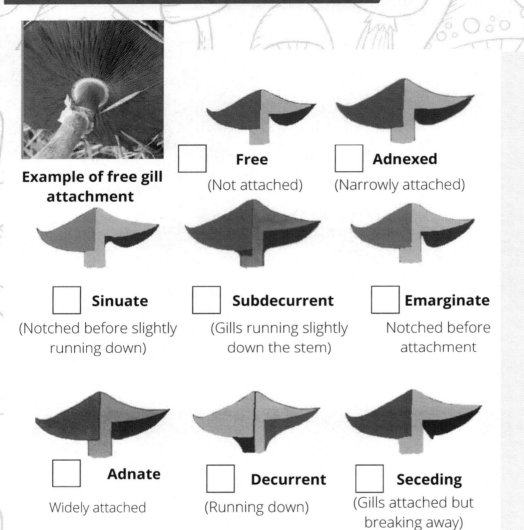

Example of free gill attachment

☐ **Free**
(Not attached)

☐ **Adnexed**
(Narrowly attached)

☐ **Sinuate**
(Notched before slightly running down)

☐ **Subdecurrent**
(Gills running slightly down the stem)

☐ **Emarginate**
Notched before attachment

☐ **Adnate**
Widely attached

☐ **Decurrent**
(Running down)

☐ **Seceding**
(Gills attached but breaking away)

Additional Notes

Stem Shape

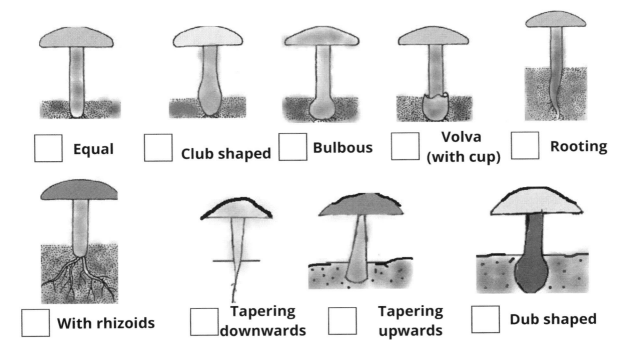

- [ ] Equal
- [ ] Club shaped
- [ ] Bulbous
- [ ] Volva (with cup)
- [ ] Rooting
- [ ] With rhizoids
- [ ] Tapering downwards
- [ ] Tapering upwards
- [ ] Dub shaped

Mushroom Ring Type

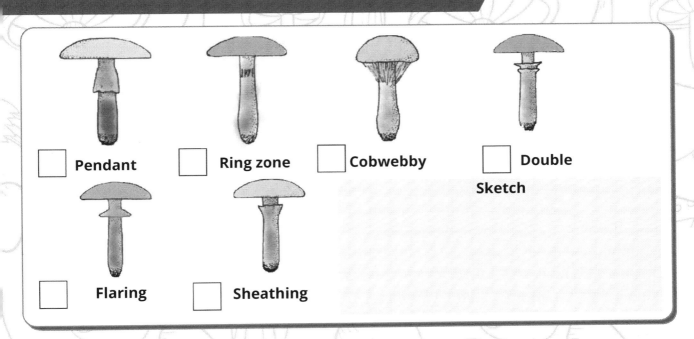

- [ ] Pendant
- [ ] Ring zone
- [ ] Cobwebby
- [ ] Double

Sketch

- [ ] Flaring
- [ ] Sheathing

Spore Print

Mushroom Species:_____

DATE: / /	**WEATHER:**	**LOCATION:**
SUBSTRATE:	Detail:	
SOIL:	**VEGETATION:**	
Recent weather:		

General Details

Date/Day _____

Weather ☐ ☐ ☐

Location/GPS _____

Temprature _____

By/Person _____

Growth Medium & Surrounding

Forest Type
☐ Coniferous ☐ Tropical ☐ Deciduous ☐ Others

Remarks _____

Growth Medium
☐ Soil ☐ Grass ☐ Dead Wood ☐ Tree
☐ Leaf ☐ Rocky Surface ☐ Mushroom ☐ Other

Remarks _____

Soil Type
☐ Clay ☐ Sandy ☐ Loam ☐ Others

Additional Information

Species/Type _____ **Color** _____

Specimen _____ **Length** _____

Cap Shape and Characterstics

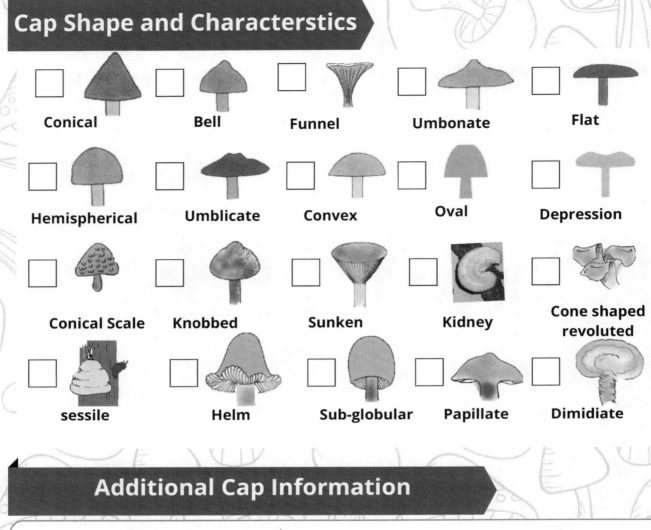

☐ Conical   ☐ Bell   ☐ Funnel   ☐ Umbonate   ☐ Flat

☐ Hemispherical   ☐ Umblicate   ☐ Convex   ☐ Oval   ☐ Depression

☐ Conical Scale   ☐ Knobbed   ☐ Sunken   ☐ Kidney   ☐ Cone shaped revoluted

☐ sessile   ☐ Helm   ☐ Sub-globular   ☐ Papillate   ☐ Dimidiate

Additional Cap Information

Cap Diagram

Other details

Cap color ....

Cap shape ....

Cap texture ....

Cap diameter ....

Cap length ....

Hymenium ....

Cap surface

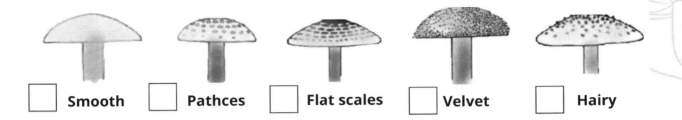

☐ Smooth   ☐ Pathces   ☐ Flat scales   ☐ Velvet   ☐ Hairy

Gills

☐ False Gills   ☐ Teeth   ☐ Pores   ☐ Gills

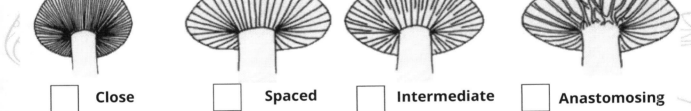

☐ Close   ☐ Spaced   ☐ Intermediate   ☐ Anastomosing

Additional Notes

Gill attachment to the stalk

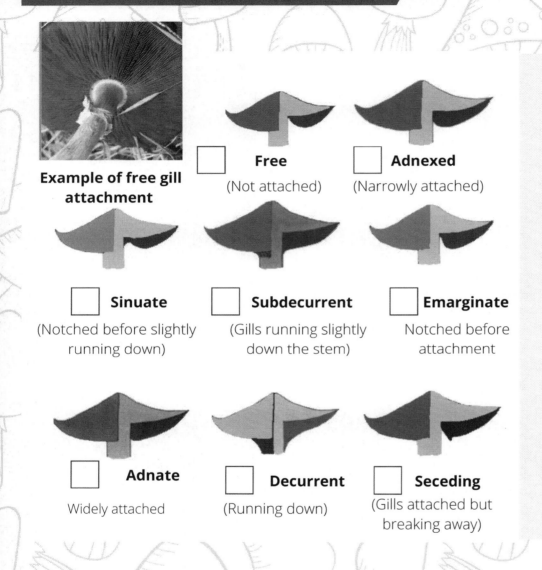

Example of free gill attachment

☐ **Free**
(Not attached)

☐ **Adnexed**
(Narrowly attached)

☐ **Sinuate**
(Notched before slightly running down)

☐ **Subdecurrent**
(Gills running slightly down the stem)

☐ **Emarginate**
Notched before attachment

☐ **Adnate**
Widely attached

☐ **Decurrent**
(Running down)

☐ **Seceding**
(Gills attached but breaking away)

Additional Notes

Stem Shape

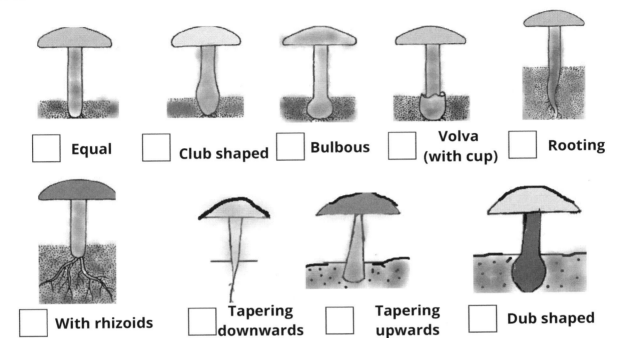

☐ Equal ☐ Club shaped ☐ Bulbous ☐ Volva (with cup) ☐ Rooting

☐ With rhizoids ☐ Tapering downwards ☐ Tapering upwards ☐ Dub shaped

Mushroom Ring Type

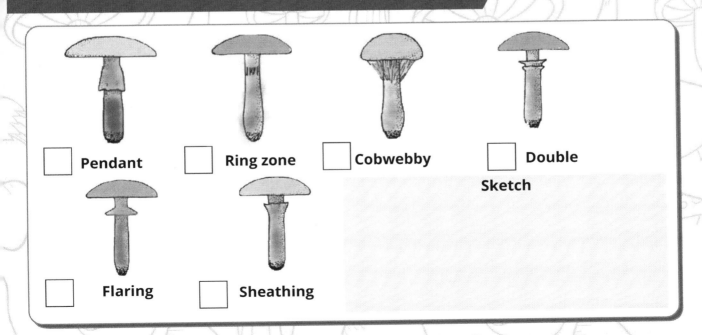

☐ Pendant ☐ Ring zone ☐ Cobwebby ☐ Double

Sketch

☐ Flaring ☐ Sheathing

Spore Print

Mushroom Species:_____

DATE: / /   **WEATHER:**   **LOCATION:**

SUBSTRATE: Detail:

SOIL: **VEGETATION:**

Recent weather:

General Details

📅 _ _ _ _ _ _ _ _ _ _ _ _ _
Date/Day

☐ ☐ ☐
Weather

📍 _ _ _ _ _ _ _ _ _ _ _ _ _
Location/GPS

🌡 _ _ _ _ _ _ _ _ _
Temprature

👤 _ _ _ _ _ _ _ _ _ _ _ _
By/Person

Growth Medium & Surrounding

☐ **Coniferous** ☐ **Tropical** ☐ **Deciduous** ☐ **Others**

Forest Type   **Remarks** _

☐ **Soil** ☐ **Grass** ☐ **Dead Wood** ☐ **Tree**

☐ **Leaf** ☐ **Rocky Surface** ☐ **Mushroom** ☐ **Other**

Growth Medium

Remarks _

☐ **Clay** ☐ **Sandy** ☐ **Loam** ☐ **Others**

Soil Type

Additional Information

Species/Type _ _ _ _ _ _ _ _ _ _ _ _ _ _ _ _ _   **Color** _ _ _ _ _ _ _ _ _ _ _ _ _ _ _ _ _

Specimen _ _ _ _ _ _ _ _ _ _ _ _ _ _ _ _ _   **Length** _ _ _ _ _ _ _ _ _ _ _ _ _ _ _ _ _

Cap Shape and Characterstics

☐ Conical ☐ Bell ☐ Funnel ☐ Umbonate ☐ Flat

☐ Hemispherical ☐ Umblicate ☐ Convex ☐ Oval ☐ Depression

☐ Conical Scale ☐ Knobbed ☐ Sunken ☐ Kidney ☐ Cone shaped revoluted

☐ sessile ☐ Helm ☐ Sub-globular ☐ Papillate ☐ Dimidiate

Additional Cap Information

Cap Diagram

Other details

Cap color ....

Cap shape ....

Cap texture ....

Cap diameter ....

Cap length ....

Hymenium ....

Cap surface

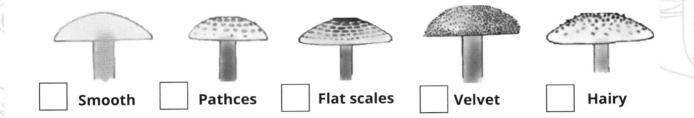

☐ Smooth ☐ Pathces ☐ Flat scales ☐ Velvet ☐ Hairy

Gills

☐ False Gills ☐ Teeth ☐ Pores ☐ Gills

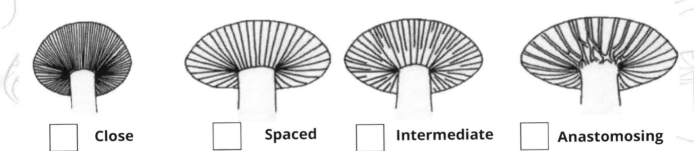

☐ Close ☐ Spaced ☐ Intermediate ☐ Anastomosing

Additional Notes

Gill attachment to the stalk

Sketch

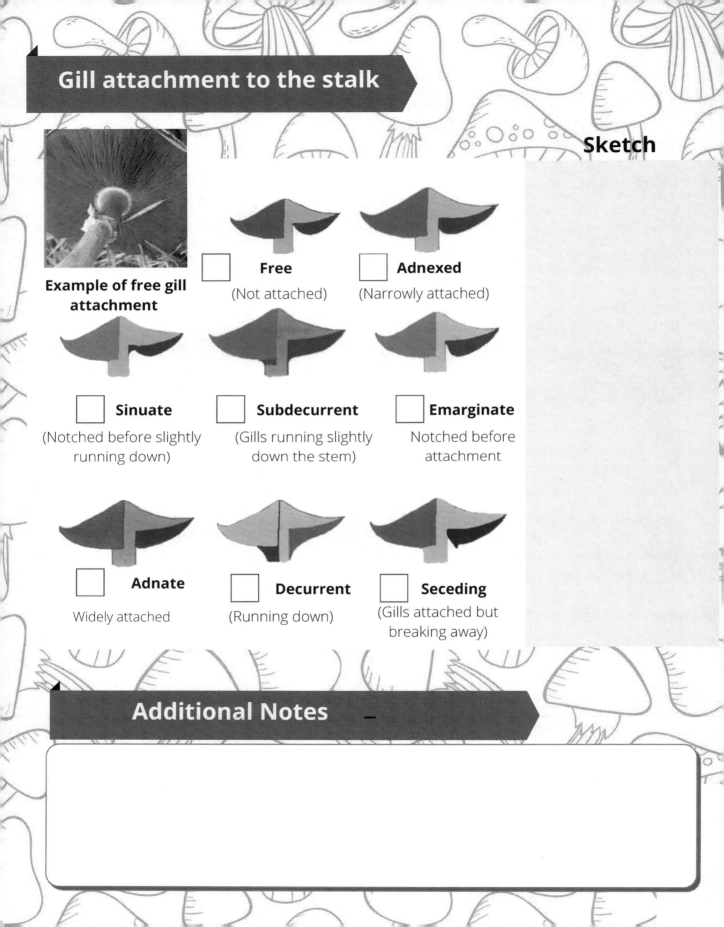

Example of free gill attachment

☐ **Free**
(Not attached)

☐ **Adnexed**
(Narrowly attached)

☐ **Sinuate**
(Notched before slightly running down)

☐ **Subdecurrent**
(Gills running slightly down the stem)

☐ **Emarginate**
Notched before attachment

☐ **Adnate**
Widely attached

☐ **Decurrent**
(Running down)

☐ **Seceding**
(Gills attached but breaking away)

Additional Notes

Stem Shape

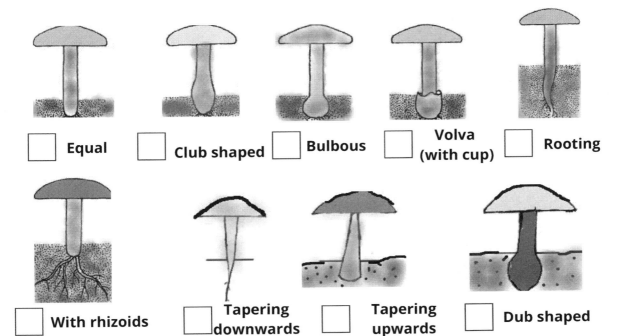

☐ Equal   ☐ Club shaped   ☐ Bulbous   ☐ Volva (with cup)   ☐ Rooting

☐ With rhizoids   ☐ Tapering downwards   ☐ Tapering upwards   ☐ Dub shaped

Mushroom Ring Type

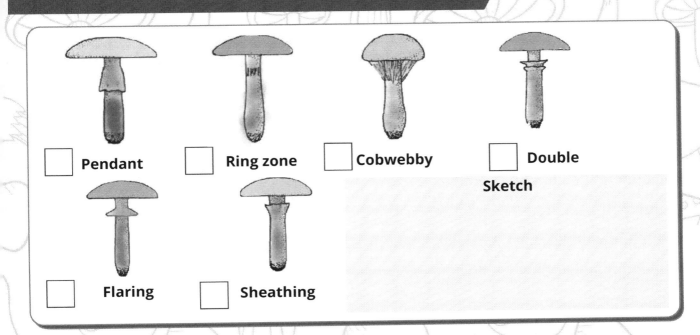

☐ Pendant   ☐ Ring zone   ☐ Cobwebby   ☐ Double

Sketch

☐ Flaring   ☐ Sheathing

Spore Print

Mushroom Species:_____

DATE: / /	WEATHER:	LOCATION:

SUBSTRATE: Detail:

SOIL: **VEGETATION:**

Recent weather:

General Details

Date/Day _____

Weather

Location/GPS _____

Temprature _____

By/Person _____

Growth Medium & Surrounding

Forest Type

☐ Coniferous ☐ Tropical ☐ Deciduous ☐ Others

Remarks _____

Growth Medium

☐ Soil ☐ Grass ☐ Dead Wood ☐ Tree

☐ Leaf ☐ Rocky Surface ☐ Mushroom ☐ Other

Remarks _____

Soil Type

☐ Clay ☐ Sandy ☐ Loam ☐ Others

Additional Information

Species/Type _____

Color _____

Specimen _____

Length _____

Cap Shape and Characterstics

☐ Conical ☐ Bell ☐ Funnel ☐ Umbonate ☐ Flat

☐ Hemispherical ☐ Umblicate ☐ Convex ☐ Oval ☐ Depression

☐ Conical Scale ☐ Knobbed ☐ Sunken ☐ Kidney ☐ Cone shaped revoluted

☐ sessile ☐ Helm ☐ Sub-globular ☐ Papillate ☐ Dimidiate

Additional Cap Information

Cap Diagram

Other details

Cap color ....

Cap shape ....

Cap texture ....

Cap diameter ....

Cap length ....

Hymenium ....

Cap surface

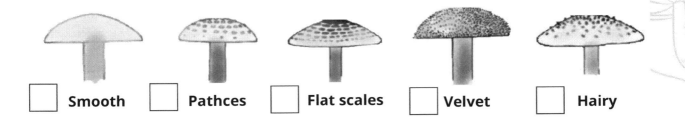

☐ Smooth ☐ Pathces ☐ Flat scales ☐ Velvet ☐ Hairy

Gills

☐ False Gills ☐ Teeth ☐ Pores ☐ Gills

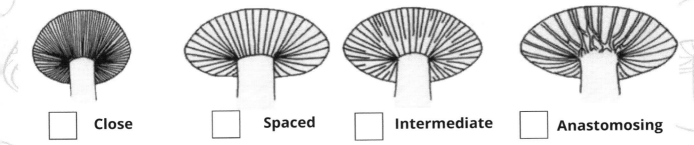

☐ Close ☐ Spaced ☐ Intermediate ☐ Anastomosing

Additional Notes

Gill attachment to the stalk

Sketch

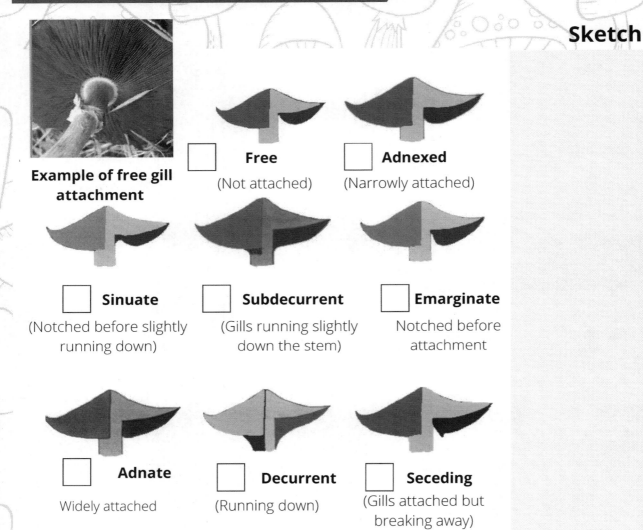

Example of free gill attachment

☐ **Free**
(Not attached)

☐ **Adnexed**
(Narrowly attached)

☐ **Sinuate**
(Notched before slightly running down)

☐ **Subdecurrent**
(Gills running slightly down the stem)

☐ **Emarginate**
Notched before attachment

☐ **Adnate**
Widely attached

☐ **Decurrent**
(Running down)

☐ **Seceding**
(Gills attached but breaking away)

Additional Notes

Stem Shape

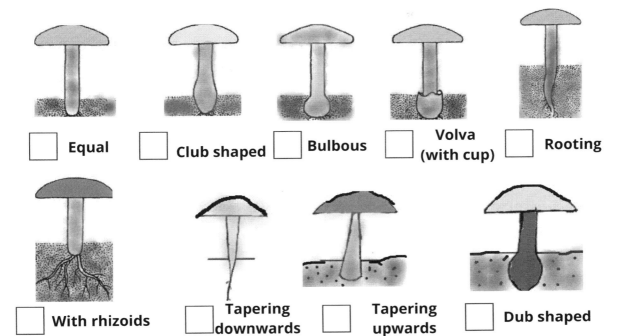

- ☐ **Equal**
- ☐ **Club shaped**
- ☐ **Bulbous**
- ☐ **Volva (with cup)**
- ☐ **Rooting**
- ☐ **With rhizoids**
- ☐ **Tapering downwards**
- ☐ **Tapering upwards**
- ☐ **Dub shaped**

Mushroom Ring Type

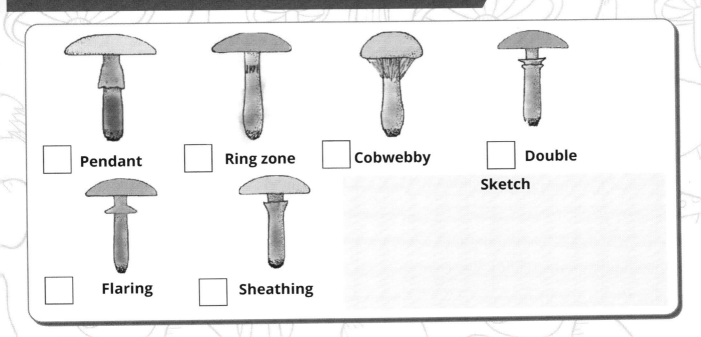

- ☐ **Pendant**
- ☐ **Ring zone**
- ☐ **Cobwebby**
- ☐ **Double**

Sketch

- ☐ **Flaring**
- ☐ **Sheathing**

Spore Print

Mushroom Species:_____

DATE: /   /   WEATHER: LOCATION:

SUBSTRATE: Detail:

SOIL: VEGETATION:

Recent weather:

General Details

Date/Day _____

Weather ☐ ☐ ☐

Location/GPS _____

Temprature _____

By/Person _____

Growth Medium & Surrounding

Forest Type

☐ Coniferous ☐ Tropical ☐ Deciduous ☐ Others

Remarks _____

Growth Medium

☐ Soil ☐ Grass ☐ Dead Wood ☐ Tree

☐ Leaf ☐ Rocky Surface ☐ Mushroom ☐ Other

Remarks _____

Soil Type

☐ Clay ☐ Sandy ☐ Loam ☐ Others

Additional Information

Species/Type _____   **Color** _____

Specimen _____   **Length** _____

Cap Shape and Characterstics

☐ Conical   ☐ Bell   ☐ Funnel   ☐ Umbonate   ☐ Flat

☐ Hemispherical   ☐ Umblicate   ☐ Convex   ☐ Oval   ☐ Depression

☐ Conical Scale   ☐ Knobbed   ☐ Sunken   ☐ Kidney   ☐ Cone shaped revoluted

☐ sessile   ☐ Helm   ☐ Sub-globular   ☐ Papillate   ☐ Dimidiate

Additional Cap Information

Cap Diagram

Other details

Cap color ....

Cap shape ....

Cap texture ....

Cap diameter ....

Cap length ....

Hymenium ....

Cap surface

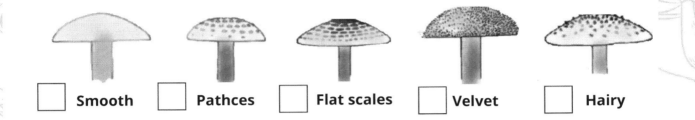

☐ Smooth ☐ Pathces ☐ Flat scales ☐ Velvet ☐ Hairy

Gills

☐ False Gills ☐ Teeth ☐ Pores ☐ Gills

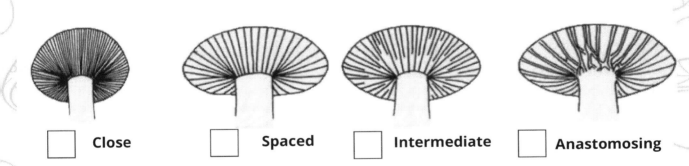

☐ Close ☐ Spaced ☐ Intermediate ☐ Anastomosing

Additional Notes

Gill attachment to the stalk

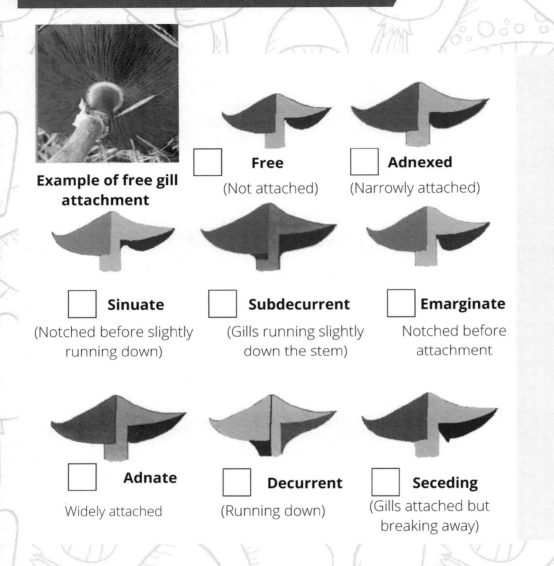

Example of free gill attachment

☐ **Free**
(Not attached)

☐ **Adnexed**
(Narrowly attached)

☐ **Sinuate**
(Notched before slightly running down)

☐ **Subdecurrent**
(Gills running slightly down the stem)

☐ **Emarginate**
Notched before attachment

☐ **Adnate**
Widely attached

☐ **Decurrent**
(Running down)

☐ **Seceding**
(Gills attached but breaking away)

Sketch

Additional Notes

Stem Shape

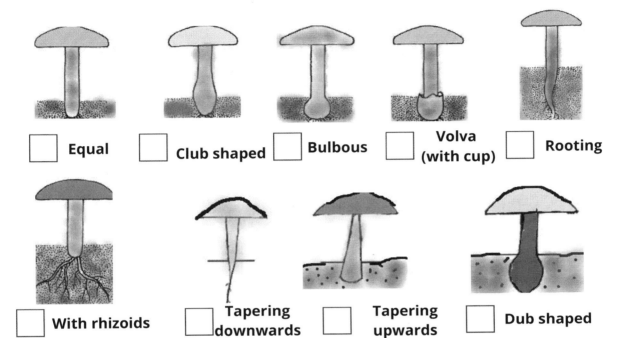

☐ Equal ☐ Club shaped ☐ Bulbous ☐ Volva (with cup) ☐ Rooting

☐ With rhizoids ☐ Tapering downwards ☐ Tapering upwards ☐ Dub shaped

Mushroom Ring Type

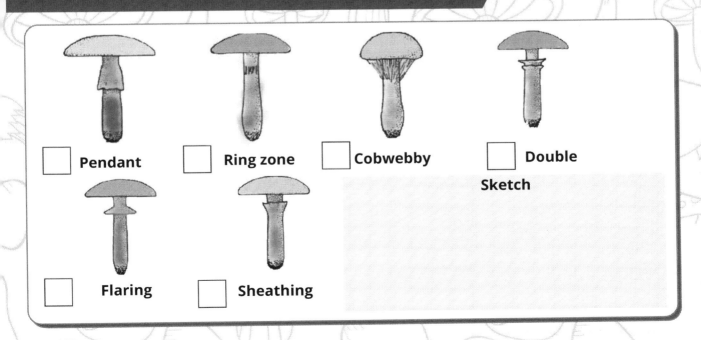

☐ Pendant ☐ Ring zone ☐ Cobwebby ☐ Double

Sketch

☐ Flaring ☐ Sheathing

Spore Print

Mushroom Species:_____

DATE: / /	WEATHER:	LOCATION:

SUBSTRATE: Detail:

SOIL: **VEGETATION:**

Recent weather:

General Details

Date/Day _____

Weather ☐ ☐ ☐

Location/GPS _____

Temprature _____

By/Person _____

Growth Medium & Surrounding

Forest Type ☐ Coniferous ☐ Tropical ☐ Deciduous ☐ Others

Remarks _____

Growth Medium
☐ Soil ☐ Grass ☐ Dead Wood ☐ Tree
☐ Leaf ☐ Rocky Surface ☐ Mushroom ☐ Other

Remarks _____

Soil Type ☐ Clay ☐ Sandy ☐ Loam ☐ Others

Additional Information

Species/Type _____

Color _____

Specimen _____

Length _____

Cap Shape and Characterstics

☐ Conical

☐ Bell

☐ Funnel

☐ Umbonate

☐ Flat

☐ Hemispherical

☐ Umblicate

☐ Convex

☐ Oval

☐ Depression

☐ Conical Scale

☐ Knobbed

☐ Sunken

☐ Kidney

☐ Cone shaped revoluted

☐ sessile

☐ Helm

☐ Sub-globular

☐ Papillate

☐ Dimidiate

Additional Cap Information

Cap Diagram

Other details

Cap color ....

Cap shape ....

Cap texture ....

Cap diameter ....

Cap length ....

Hymenium ....

Cap surface

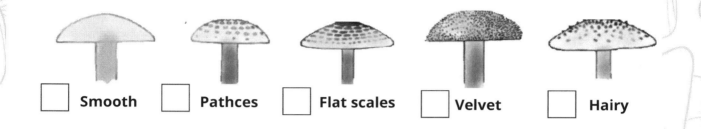

- ☐ Smooth
- ☐ Pathces
- ☐ Flat scales
- ☐ Velvet
- ☐ Hairy

Gills

- ☐ False Gills
- ☐ Teeth
- ☐ Pores
- ☐ Gills

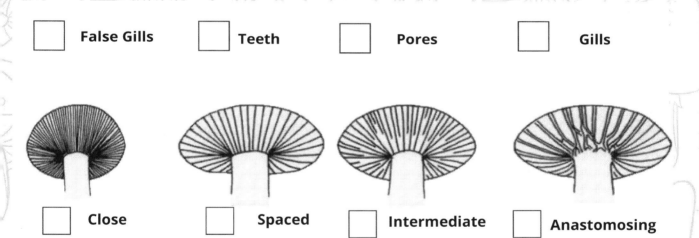

- ☐ Close
- ☐ Spaced
- ☐ Intermediate
- ☐ Anastomosing

Additional Notes

Gill attachment to the stalk

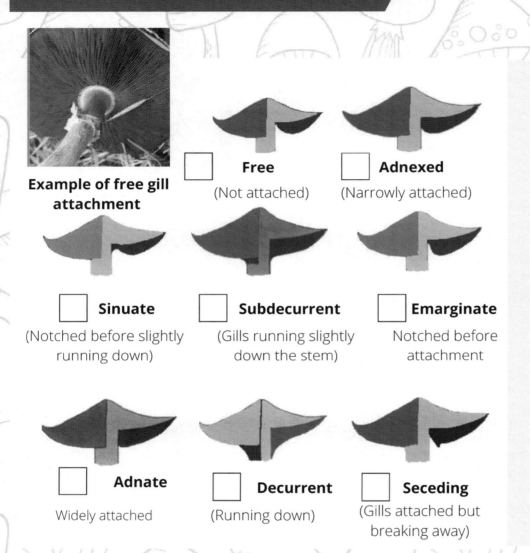

Example of free gill attachment

☐ **Free**
(Not attached)

☐ **Adnexed**
(Narrowly attached)

☐ **Sinuate**
(Notched before slightly running down)

☐ **Subdecurrent**
(Gills running slightly down the stem)

☐ **Emarginate**
Notched before attachment

☐ **Adnate**
Widely attached

☐ **Decurrent**
(Running down)

☐ **Seceding**
(Gills attached but breaking away)

Sketch

Additional Notes

Stem Shape

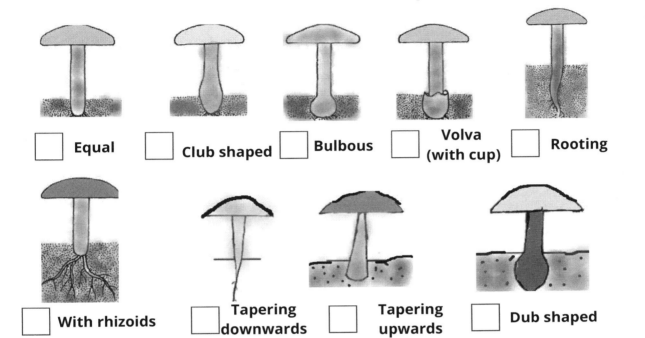

☐ Equal ☐ Club shaped ☐ Bulbous ☐ Volva (with cup) ☐ Rooting

☐ With rhizoids ☐ Tapering downwards ☐ Tapering upwards ☐ Dub shaped

Mushroom Ring Type

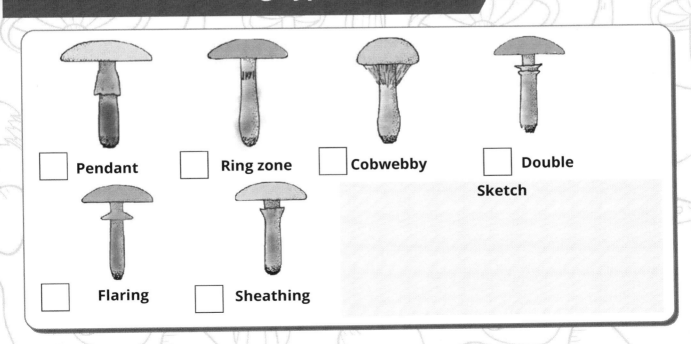

☐ Pendant ☐ Ring zone ☐ Cobwebby ☐ Double

Sketch

☐ Flaring ☐ Sheathing

Spore Print

Mushroom Species:_____

DATE: / /   **WEATHER:**   **LOCATION:**

SUBSTRATE: Detail:

SOIL: **VEGETATION:**

Recent weather:

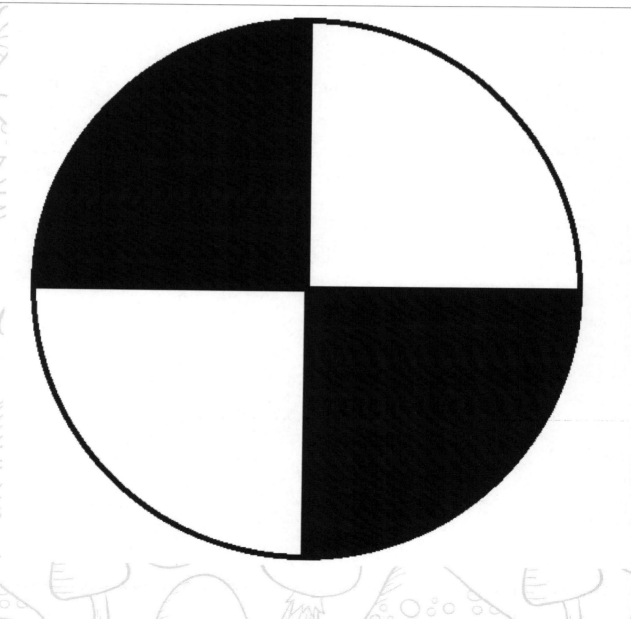

General Details

Date/Day _____

Weather ☐ ☐ ☐

Location/GPS _____

Temprature _____

By/Person _____

Growth Medium & Surrounding

Forest Type

☐ Coniferous ☐ Tropical ☐ Deciduous ☐ Others

Remarks _____

Growth Medium

☐ Soil ☐ Grass ☐ Dead Wood ☐ Tree

☐ Leaf ☐ Rocky Surface ☐ Mushroom ☐ Other

Remarks _____

Soil Type

☐ Clay ☐ Sandy ☐ Loam ☐ Others

Additional Information

Species/Type _____

Color _____

Specimen _____

Length _____

Cap Shape and Characterstics

☐ Conical
☐ Bell
☐ Funnel
☐ Umbonate
☐ Flat

☐ Hemispherical
☐ Umblicate
☐ Convex
☐ Oval
☐ Depression

☐ Conical Scale
☐ Knobbed
☐ Sunken
☐ Kidney
☐ Cone shaped revoluted

☐ sessile
☐ Helm
☐ Sub-globular
☐ Papillate
☐ Dimidiate

Additional Cap Information

Cap Diagram

Other details

Cap color ....

Cap shape ....

Cap texture ....

Cap diameter ....

Cap length ....

Hymenium ....

Cap surface

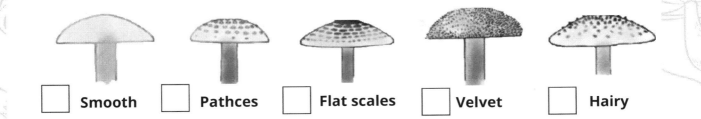

- ☐ Smooth
- ☐ Pathces
- ☐ Flat scales
- ☐ Velvet
- ☐ Hairy

Gills

- ☐ False Gills
- ☐ Teeth
- ☐ Pores
- ☐ Gills

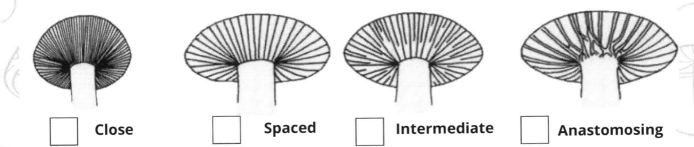

- ☐ Close
- ☐ Spaced
- ☐ Intermediate
- ☐ Anastomosing

Additional Notes

Gill attachment to the stalk

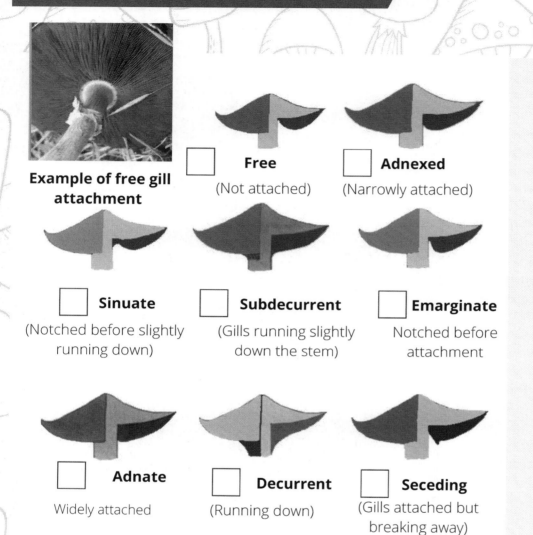

Example of free gill attachment

☐ **Free**
(Not attached)

☐ **Adnexed**
(Narrowly attached)

☐ **Sinuate**
(Notched before slightly running down)

☐ **Subdecurrent**
(Gills running slightly down the stem)

☐ **Emarginate**
Notched before attachment

☐ **Adnate**
Widely attached

☐ **Decurrent**
(Running down)

☐ **Seceding**
(Gills attached but breaking away)

Sketch

Additional Notes

Stem Shape

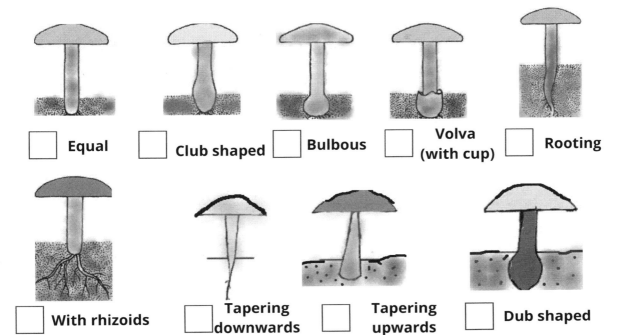

☐ Equal ☐ Club shaped ☐ Bulbous ☐ Volva (with cup) ☐ Rooting

☐ With rhizoids ☐ Tapering downwards ☐ Tapering upwards ☐ Dub shaped

Mushroom Ring Type

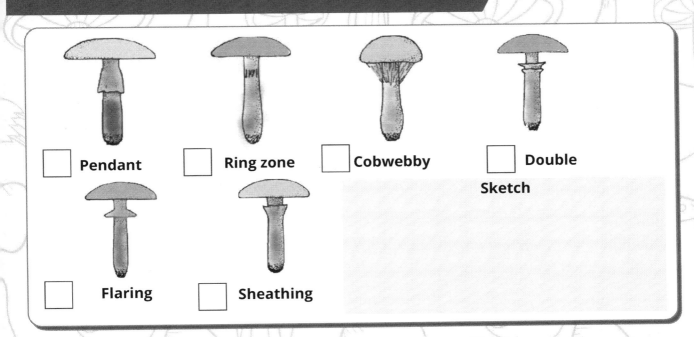

☐ Pendant ☐ Ring zone ☐ Cobwebby ☐ Double

Sketch

☐ Flaring ☐ Sheathing

Spore Print

Mushroom Species: _____

DATE: / /	**WEATHER:**	**LOCATION:**
SUBSTRATE:	**Detail:**	
SOIL:	**VEGETATION:**	
Recent weather:		

General Details

Date/Day _____

Weather ☐ ☐ ☐ ☐

Location/GPS _____

Temprature _____

By/Person _____

Growth Medium & Surrounding

Forest Type

☐ Coniferous ☐ Tropical ☐ Deciduous ☐ Others

Remarks _____

Growth Medium

☐ Soil ☐ Grass ☐ Dead Wood ☐ Tree

☐ Leaf ☐ Rocky Surface ☐ Mushroom ☐ Other

Remarks _____

Soil Type

☐ Clay ☐ Sandy ☐ Loam ☐ Others

Additional Information

Species/Type _____   **Color** _____

Specimen _____   **Length** _____

Cap Shape and Characterstics

☐ Conical

☐ Bell

☐ Funnel

☐ Umbonate

☐ Flat

☐ Hemispherical

☐ Umblicate

☐ Convex

☐ Oval

☐ Depression

☐ Conical Scale

☐ Knobbed

☐ Sunken

☐ Kidney

☐ Cone shaped revoluted

☐ sessile

☐ Helm

☐ Sub-globular

☐ Papillate

☐ Dimidiate

Additional Cap Information

Cap Diagram

Other details

Cap color ....

Cap shape ....

Cap texture ....

Cap diameter ....

Cap length ....

Hymenium ....

Cap surface

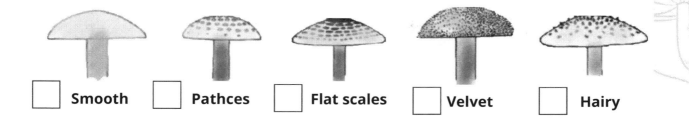

☐ Smooth   ☐ Pathces   ☐ Flat scales   ☐ Velvet   ☐ Hairy

Gills

☐ False Gills   ☐ Teeth   ☐ Pores   ☐ Gills

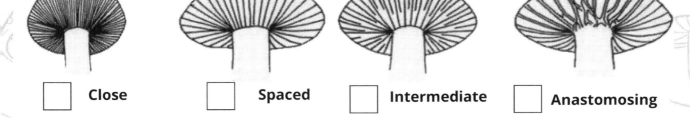

☐ Close   ☐ Spaced   ☐ Intermediate   ☐ Anastomosing

Additional Notes

Gill attachment to the stalk

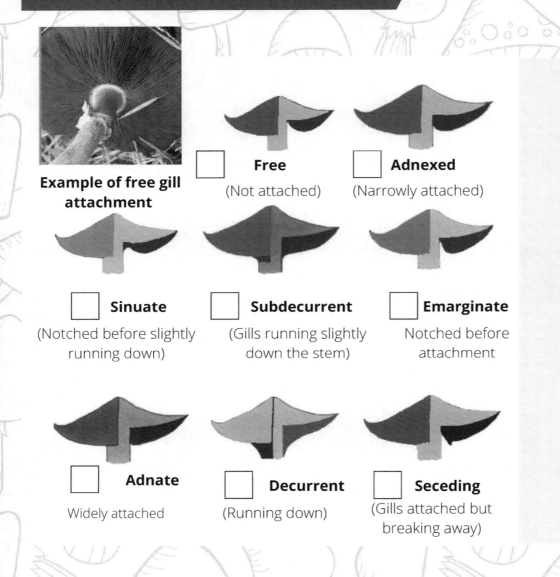

Example of free gill attachment

☐ **Free**
(Not attached)

☐ **Adnexed**
(Narrowly attached)

☐ **Sinuate**
(Notched before slightly running down)

☐ **Subdecurrent**
(Gills running slightly down the stem)

☐ **Emarginate**
Notched before attachment

☐ **Adnate**
Widely attached

☐ **Decurrent**
(Running down)

☐ **Seceding**
(Gills attached but breaking away)

Sketch

Additional Notes

Stem Shape

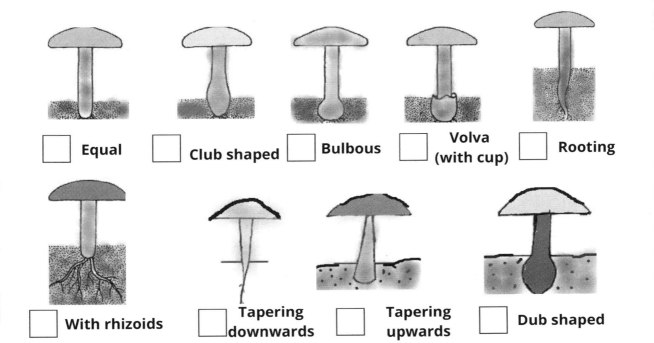

[ ] Equal   [ ] Club shaped   [ ] Bulbous   [ ] Volva (with cup)   [ ] Rooting

[ ] With rhizoids   [ ] Tapering downwards   [ ] Tapering upwards   [ ] Dub shaped

Mushroom Ring Type

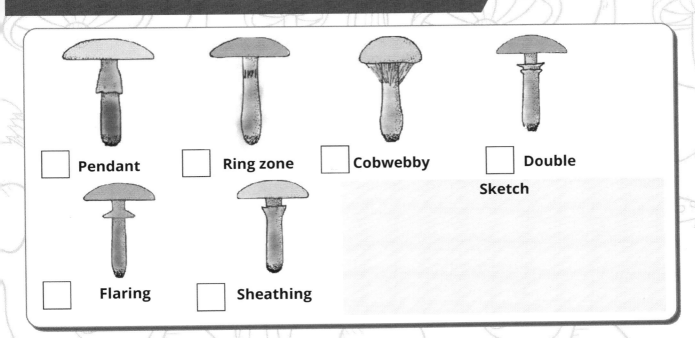

[ ] Pendant   [ ] Ring zone   [ ] Cobwebby   [ ] Double

Sketch

[ ] Flaring   [ ] Sheathing

Spore Print

Mushroom Species:_____

DATE: / /	WEATHER:	LOCATION:

SUBSTRATE: Detail:

SOIL: **VEGETATION:**

Recent weather:

General Details

Date/Day _ _ _ _ _ _ _ _ _ _ _ _

Weather ☐ ☐ ☐

Location/GPS _ _ _ _ _ _ _ _ _ _ _ _

Temprature _ _ _ _ _ _ _ _ _

By/Person _ _ _ _ _ _ _ _ _

Growth Medium & Surrounding

Forest Type

☐ Coniferous ☐ Tropical ☐ Deciduous ☐ Others

Remarks _

Growth Medium

☐ Soil ☐ Grass ☐ Dead Wood ☐ Tree

☐ Leaf ☐ Rocky Surface ☐ Mushroom ☐ Other

Remarks _

Soil Type

☐ Clay ☐ Sandy ☐ Loam ☐ Others

Additional Information

Species/Type _ _ _ _ _ _ _ _ _ _ _ _ _ _ _ _

Color _ _ _ _ _ _ _ _ _ _ _ _ _ _ _ _

Specimen _ _ _ _ _ _ _ _ _ _ _ _ _ _ _ _

Length _ _ _ _ _ _ _ _ _ _ _ _ _ _ _ _

Cap Shape and Characterstics

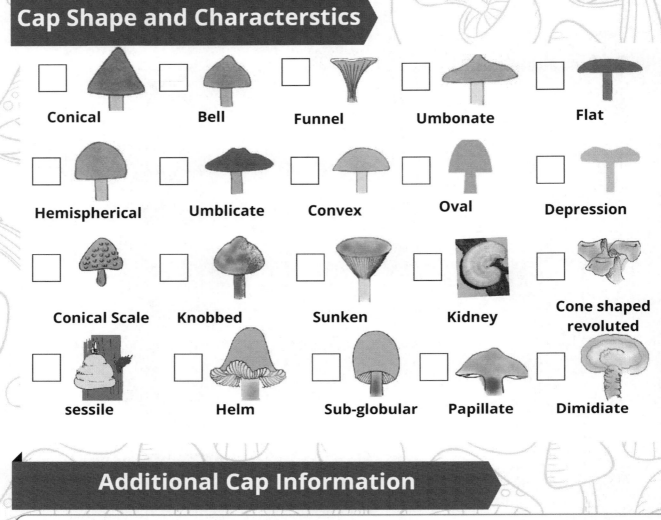

☐ Conical   ☐ Bell   ☐ Funnel   ☐ Umbonate   ☐ Flat

☐ Hemispherical   ☐ Umblicate   ☐ Convex   ☐ Oval   ☐ Depression

☐ Conical Scale   ☐ Knobbed   ☐ Sunken   ☐ Kidney   ☐ Cone shaped revoluted

☐ sessile   ☐ Helm   ☐ Sub-globular   ☐ Papillate   ☐ Dimidiate

Additional Cap Information

Cap Diagram

Other details

Cap color ....

Cap shape ....

Cap texture ....

Cap diameter ....

Cap length ....

Hymenium ....

Cap surface

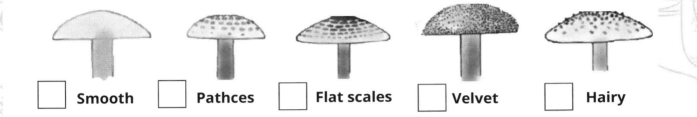

☐ Smooth ☐ Pathces ☐ Flat scales ☐ Velvet ☐ Hairy

Gills

☐ False Gills ☐ Teeth ☐ Pores ☐ Gills

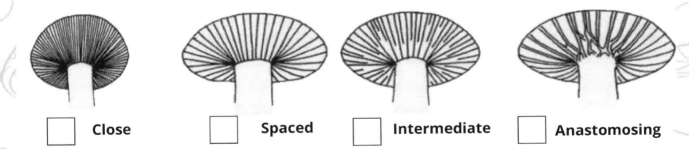

☐ Close ☐ Spaced ☐ Intermediate ☐ Anastomosing

Additional Notes

Gill attachment to the stalk

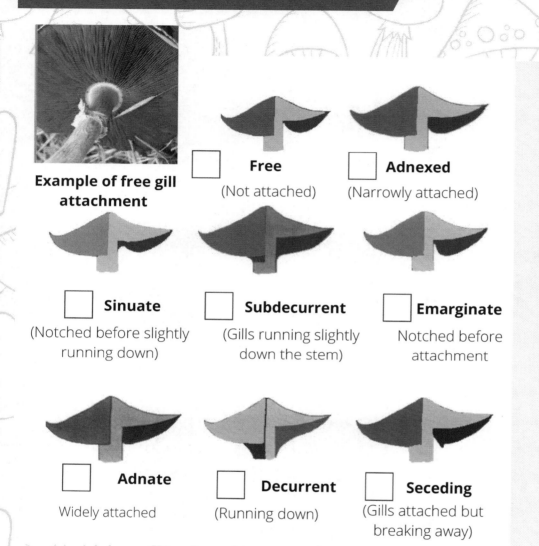

Example of free gill attachment

☐ **Free**
(Not attached)

☐ **Adnexed**
(Narrowly attached)

☐ **Sinuate**
(Notched before slightly running down)

☐ **Subdecurrent**
(Gills running slightly down the stem)

☐ **Emarginate**
Notched before attachment

☐ **Adnate**
Widely attached

☐ **Decurrent**
(Running down)

☐ **Seceding**
(Gills attached but breaking away)

Sketch

Additional Notes

Stem Shape

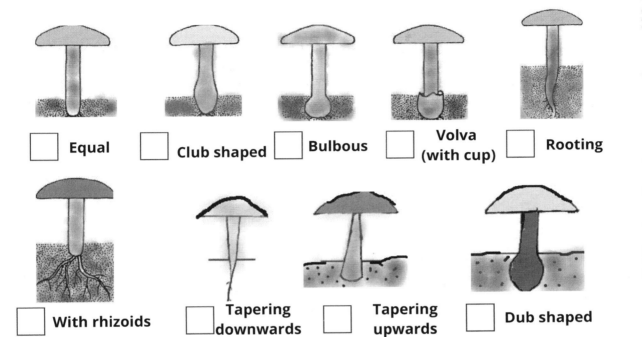

- [ ] Equal
- [ ] Club shaped
- [ ] Bulbous
- [ ] Volva (with cup)
- [ ] Rooting
- [ ] With rhizoids
- [ ] Tapering downwards
- [ ] Tapering upwards
- [ ] Dub shaped

Mushroom Ring Type

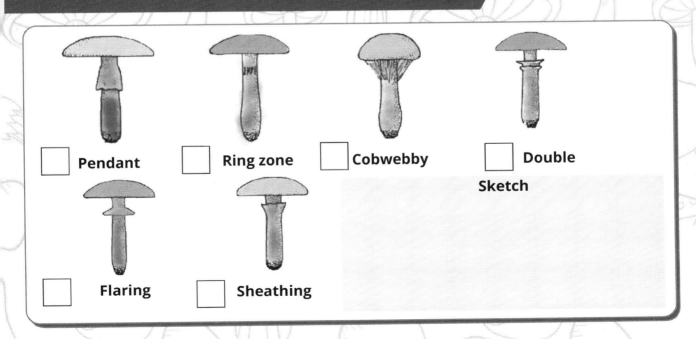

- [ ] Pendant
- [ ] Ring zone
- [ ] Cobwebby
- [ ] Double
- [ ] Flaring
- [ ] Sheathing

Sketch

Spore Print

Mushroom Species:_____

DATE: / /	WEATHER:	LOCATION:

SUBSTRATE: Detail:

SOIL: **VEGETATION:**

Recent weather:

General Details

Date/Day _____

Weather

Location/GPS _____

Temprature _____

By/Person _____

Growth Medium & Surrounding

Forest Type

☐ Coniferous   ☐ Tropical   ☐ Deciduous   ☐ Others

Remarks _____

Growth Medium

☐ Soil   ☐ Grass   ☐ Dead Wood   ☐ Tree

☐ Leaf   ☐ Rocky Surface   ☐ Mushroom   ☐ Other

Remarks _____

Soil Type

☐ Clay   ☐ Sandy   ☐ Loam   ☐ Others

Additional Information

Species/Type _____   **Color** _____

Specimen _____   **Length** _____

Cap Shape and Characterstics

☐ Conical

☐ Bell

☐ Funnel

☐ Umbonate

☐ Flat

☐ Hemispherical

☐ Umblicate

☐ Convex

☐ Oval

☐ Depression

☐ Conical Scale

☐ Knobbed

☐ Sunken

☐ Kidney

☐ Cone shaped revoluted

☐ sessile

☐ Helm

☐ Sub-globular

☐ Papillate

☐ Dimidiate

Additional Cap Information

Cap Diagram

Other details

Cap color ....

Cap shape ....

Cap texture ....

Cap diameter ....

Cap length ....

Hymenium ....

Cap surface

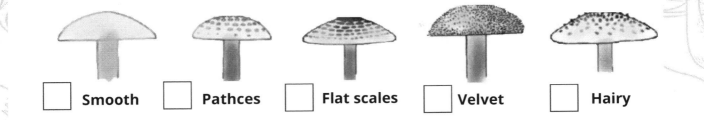

☐ Smooth ☐ Pathces ☐ Flat scales ☐ Velvet ☐ Hairy

Gills

☐ False Gills ☐ Teeth ☐ Pores ☐ Gills

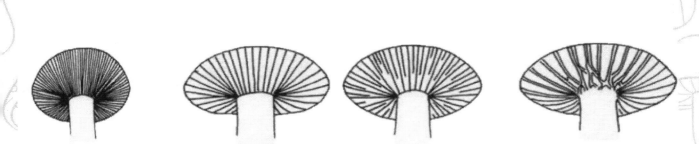

☐ Close ☐ Spaced ☐ Intermediate ☐ Anastomosing

Additional Notes

Gill attachment to the stalk

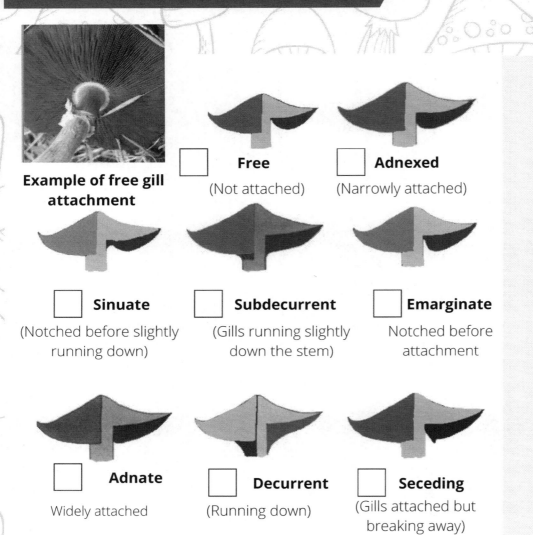

Example of free gill attachment

☐ **Free**
(Not attached)

☐ **Adnexed**
(Narrowly attached)

☐ **Sinuate**
(Notched before slightly running down)

☐ **Subdecurrent**
(Gills running slightly down the stem)

☐ **Emarginate**
Notched before attachment

☐ **Adnate**
Widely attached

☐ **Decurrent**
(Running down)

☐ **Seceding**
(Gills attached but breaking away)

Sketch

Additional Notes

Stem Shape

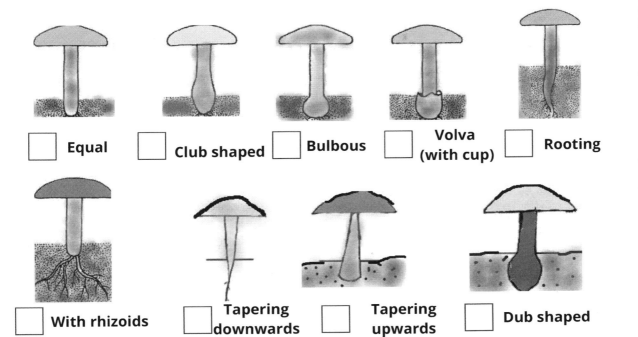

- ☐ **Equal**
- ☐ **Club shaped**
- ☐ **Bulbous**
- ☐ **Volva (with cup)**
- ☐ **Rooting**
- ☐ **With rhizoids**
- ☐ **Tapering downwards**
- ☐ **Tapering upwards**
- ☐ **Dub shaped**

Mushroom Ring Type

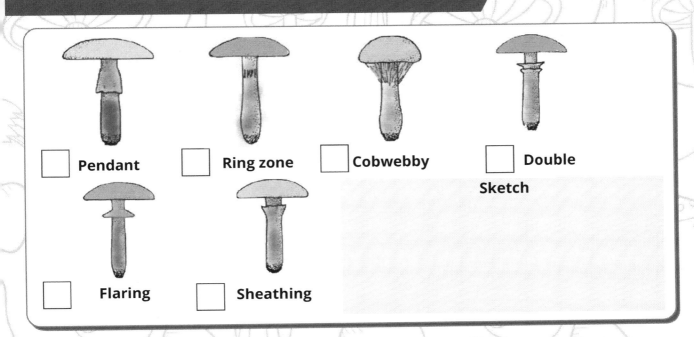

- ☐ **Pendant**
- ☐ **Ring zone**
- ☐ **Cobwebby**
- ☐ **Double**
- ☐ **Flaring**
- ☐ **Sheathing**

Sketch

Spore Print

Mushroom Species:_____

DATE: / /   **WEATHER:**   **LOCATION:**

SUBSTRATE: Detail:

SOIL: **VEGETATION:**

Recent weather:

General Details

Date/Day _____

Weather

Location/GPS _____

Temprature _____

By/Person _____

Growth Medium & Surrounding

Forest Type

- [ ] Coniferous
- [ ] Tropical
- [ ] Deciduous
- [ ] Others

Remarks _____

Growth Medium

- [ ] Soil
- [ ] Grass
- [ ] Dead Wood
- [ ] Tree
- [ ] Leaf
- [ ] Rocky Surface
- [ ] Mushroom
- [ ] Other

Remarks _____

Soil Type

- [ ] Clay
- [ ] Sandy
- [ ] Loam
- [ ] Others

Additional Information

Species/Type _____

Color _____

Specimen _____

Length _____

Cap Shape and Characterstics

☐ Conical

☐ Bell

☐ Funnel

☐ Umbonate

☐ Flat

☐ Hemispherical

☐ Umblicate

☐ Convex

☐ Oval

☐ Depression

☐ Conical Scale

☐ Knobbed

☐ Sunken

☐ Kidney

☐ Cone shaped revoluted

☐ sessile

☐ Helm

☐ Sub-globular

☐ Papillate

☐ Dimidiate

Additional Cap Information

Cap Diagram

Other details

Cap color ....

Cap shape ....

Cap texture ....

Cap diameter ....

Cap length ....

Hymenium ....

Cap surface

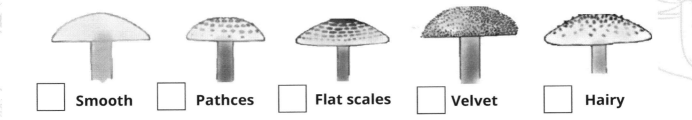

- ☐ Smooth
- ☐ Pathces
- ☐ Flat scales
- ☐ Velvet
- ☐ Hairy

Gills

- ☐ False Gills
- ☐ Teeth
- ☐ Pores
- ☐ Gills

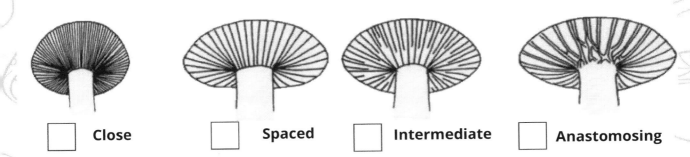

- ☐ Close
- ☐ Spaced
- ☐ Intermediate
- ☐ Anastomosing

Additional Notes

Gill attachment to the stalk

Sketch

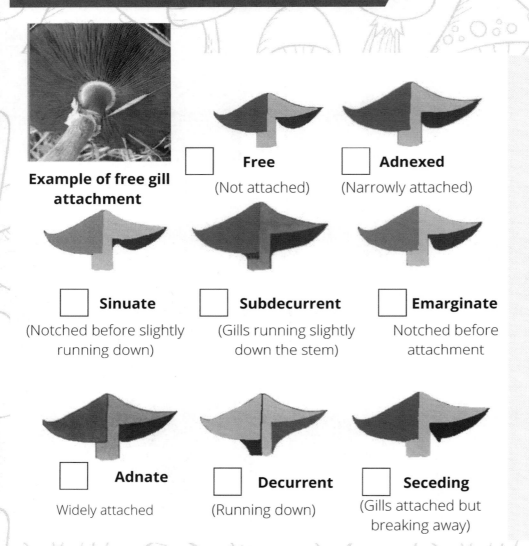

Example of free gill attachment

☐ **Free**
(Not attached)

☐ **Adnexed**
(Narrowly attached)

☐ **Sinuate**
(Notched before slightly running down)

☐ **Subdecurrent**
(Gills running slightly down the stem)

☐ **Emarginate**
Notched before attachment

☐ **Adnate**
Widely attached

☐ **Decurrent**
(Running down)

☐ **Seceding**
(Gills attached but breaking away)

Additional Notes

Stem Shape

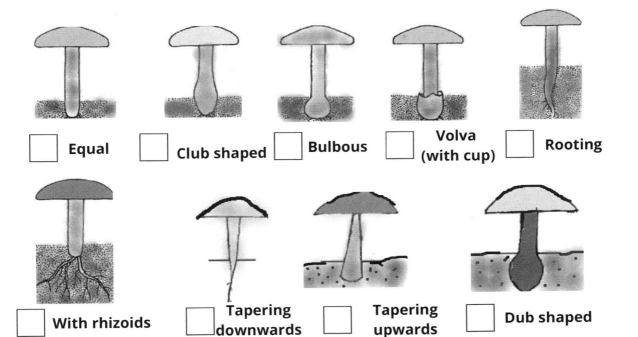

- ☐ Equal
- ☐ Club shaped
- ☐ Bulbous
- ☐ Volva (with cup)
- ☐ Rooting
- ☐ With rhizoids
- ☐ Tapering downwards
- ☐ Tapering upwards
- ☐ Dub shaped

Mushroom Ring Type

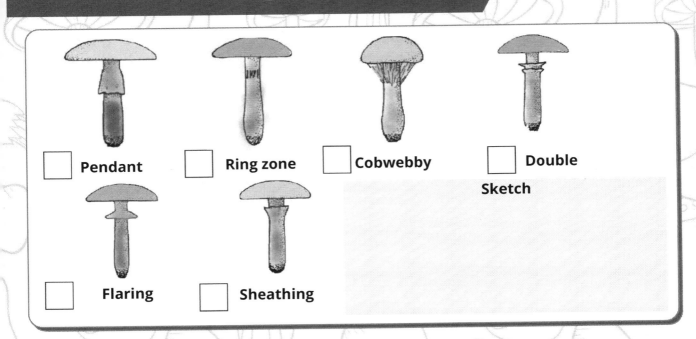

- ☐ Pendant
- ☐ Ring zone
- ☐ Cobwebby
- ☐ Double

Sketch

- ☐ Flaring
- ☐ Sheathing

Spore Print

Mushroom Species:_____

DATE: / /	WEATHER:	LOCATION:

SUBSTRATE: Detail:

SOIL: **VEGETATION:**

Recent weather:

General Details

Date/Day _____

Weather ☐ ☐ ☐

Location/GPS _____

Temprature _____

By/Person _____

Growth Medium & Surrounding

Forest Type
☐ Coniferous ☐ Tropical ☐ Deciduous ☐ Others

Remarks _____

Growth Medium
☐ Soil ☐ Grass ☐ Dead Wood ☐ Tree
☐ Leaf ☐ Rocky Surface ☐ Mushroom ☐ Other

Remarks _____

Soil Type
☐ Clay ☐ Sandy ☐ Loam ☐ Others

Additional Information

Species/Type _____

Color _____

Specimen _____

Length _____

Cap Shape and Characterstics

- [ ] Conical
- [ ] Bell
- [ ] Funnel
- [ ] Umbonate
- [ ] Flat

- [ ] Hemispherical
- [ ] Umblicate
- [ ] Convex
- [ ] Oval
- [ ] Depression

- [ ] Conical Scale
- [ ] Knobbed
- [ ] Sunken
- [ ] Kidney
- [ ] Cone shaped revoluted

- [ ] sessile
- [ ] Helm
- [ ] Sub-globular
- [ ] Papillate
- [ ] Dimidiate

Additional Cap Information

Cap Diagram

Other details

Cap color ....

Cap shape ....

Cap texture ....

Cap diameter ....

Cap length ....

Hymenium ....

Cap surface

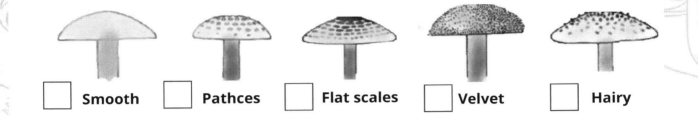

☐ Smooth   ☐ Pathces   ☐ Flat scales   ☐ Velvet   ☐ Hairy

Gills

☐ False Gills   ☐ Teeth   ☐ Pores   ☐ Gills

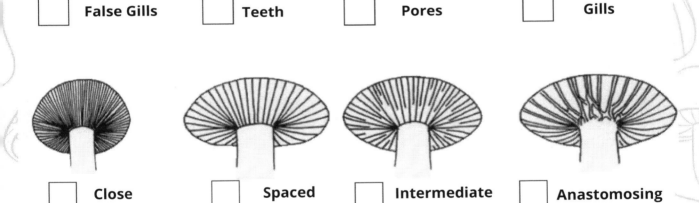

☐ Close   ☐ Spaced   ☐ Intermediate   ☐ Anastomosing

Additional Notes

Gill attachment to the stalk

Sketch

Example of free gill attachment

☐ **Free**
(Not attached)

☐ **Adnexed**
(Narrowly attached)

☐ **Sinuate**
(Notched before slightly running down)

☐ **Subdecurrent**
(Gills running slightly down the stem)

☐ **Emarginate**
Notched before attachment

☐ **Adnate**
Widely attached

☐ **Decurrent**
(Running down)

☐ **Seceding**
(Gills attached but breaking away)

Additional Notes

Stem Shape

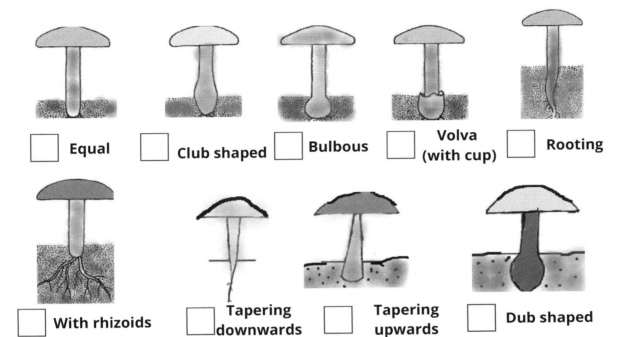

- [ ] Equal
- [ ] Club shaped
- [ ] Bulbous
- [ ] Volva (with cup)
- [ ] Rooting
- [ ] With rhizoids
- [ ] Tapering downwards
- [ ] Tapering upwards
- [ ] Dub shaped

Mushroom Ring Type

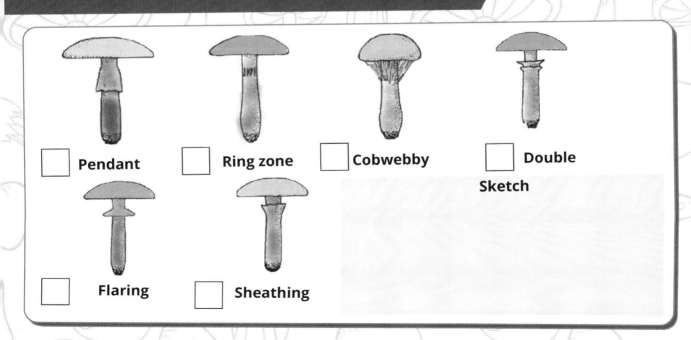

- [ ] Pendant
- [ ] Ring zone
- [ ] Cobwebby
- [ ] Double

Sketch

- [ ] Flaring
- [ ] Sheathing

Spore Print

Mushroom Species:_____

| DATE: / / | WEATHER: | LOCATION: |

SUBSTRATE: Detail:

SOIL: VEGETATION:

Recent weather:

Glossary

Mycelia: Mycelium is the underground part of the fungus. It is composed of hyphae, which look like strings or rootlets. The floor covering of hyphae may be thickly woven. Its main feature is to extract nutrients. Fungal nests made up of mycelium are located on soil and many other natural products called substrates.

Substrate: The surface area or material on or from which a microorganism lives grows or acquires its sustenance.

Spores: Tiny, single-celled devices created by mushrooms in the process of sexual reproduction-- roughly comparable to seeds.

Gills: Plate-like or blade-like frameworks attached to the underside of the cap in lots of participants of the Basidiomycota

Tubes: Numerous mushrooms such as bolete and polypore use tubes, not gills, to deliver spores.

Mycorrhizal: Mycorrhizal Mushrooms are associated with an equally beneficial partnership with the rootlets of plants-- generally trees.

Cap: The top part of a mushroom opens up as it develops and where the spore-producing cells lie.

Fruiting body: The fruiting body is the reproductive organ of fungi that spreads its spores, formed by pressed mycelium that grows exterior from the growing tool. For most edible varieties of fungi, the fruiting body is the actual mushroom.

Gill: The spore-bearing part of a mushroom, usually situated beneath the cap. Most typical edible mushrooms have gills, yet some have pores.

Pin: A tiny, undeveloped mushroom, named so since it typically appears like a bit of pin. Pins are also called primordia. When pins create, it's called pinning or fruiting. After that, pins will rapidly grow into huge, full-sized mushrooms.

Pore: The spore-bearing part of a mushroom, generally situated beneath the cap. Most typical edible mushrooms do not have pores; some do, such as wild porcini mushrooms.

Spawn: Spawn is a society of fungal mycelium grown on a growing tool. One of the most common spawn substrates is grain spawn, containing damp, cooked grains that permit mycelium to proliferate. In addition, spawn can be used to fruit mushrooms straight or like seeds to inoculate more growing media such as logs, wood chips, manure, or sawdust.

Spore Print: Spore prints are the pattern of spores left on a sheet of paper, foil, or glass when a fully grown mushroom cap is positioned on it uninterrupted for several hours, approximately a day. Spore prints can be utilized to assist in identifying the types of mushrooms (integrated with various other features) as various mushrooms will have various patterns and colors of spore prints. Spore prints can additionally be made use of to accumulate spores to grow mushrooms.

Veil: The thin membrane that attaches a creating mushroom cap to the stalk. When the mushroom cap opens, the veil breaks. Some types of mushrooms have a ring around the stalk where the veil was when connected.

Other Poisnous Mushrooms

**Podostroma Cornu-damae/
Poison fire coral**

Fool's Mushroom/Amanita verna

**Ivory Funnel/
Clitocybe dealbata**

**Deadly Dapperling /
Lepiota brunneoincarnata**

Poisnous Mushrooms		
Name	**Body part affected**	**Found in**
Asian Abrupt-Bulbed Lepidella	Liver and Kidney	Woods of Eastern Asia
Autumn Skullcap	Liver	Worldwide
Brown Roll-Rim	Rupturing of Red Blood Cells	Europe and North America
Deadly Dapperling	Liver	Woods of Europe
Deadly Webcap	Kidney	Woods of Northern Europe
Death Cap	Liver and Upper Gastrointestinal Tract	Woods of Europe, North Africa, North America, Australia, New Zealand
False Morel	Kidney,Liver and other	Woods of the Northern Hemisphere
Ivory Funnel	Central Nervous System	Europe and North America

Carry below items

- **Notepad**
- **Magnifying Glass**
- **Mushroom Cutting Knife**
- **Basket**
- **Headlamp**
- **Boot and Waterproof clothes**
- **Local Map**
- **GPS**
- **A small stick**

IDENTIFY MUSHROOMS

Notes

_____

_____

_____

_____

_____

_____

_____

Notes

_____

_____

_____

_____

_____

_____

_____

Notes

_____

_____

_____

_____

_____

_____

_____

Notes

_____

_____

_____

_____

_____

_____

_____

Sketch/Diagram

Sketch/Diagram

Sketch/Diagram

Sketch/Diagram

Sketch/Diagram

Made in United States
Orlando, FL
21 December 2021